MIND BLOWING HISTORICAL FACTS!

BY
Akiba Rakilam

ACKNOWLEDGEMENTS

I would like to take this time to t hank all of my brothers and sisters whom are laboring to build the temple, as well as Gwen Thomas and Abika Rakilam for assisting me in my life endeavors. Special acknowledgement goes to Antonio Davis for his analytical critique in regards to the construction of this book, T. McDaniel, Chike Rakilam, Sa'id Rakilam, Kathy Crogg, , Reggie "RAPPA'. Mikyas Gernachew, Tanita Hightower, Darrick Evans, Wayne Clipper, Majestic, Prophecy (Bush-EL), Lolita, Poodie, Fatima, Tony Taylor, Rosa Gerola, Larry H., Dorenda Reed for her sedulous support in regards to my projects, Barbara, Latoya Brooks, Philson-EL, Shawn White-EL, Harry Ellis, Tasha, Mia Reed, Mr. Joseph Thomas, Bilal, Tanisha, Bowman-Bey, Tim White, Vernon Mills-EL, Dante Bailey, Jahbazz Whatley, Destiny Whatley, Scoop for his real live assistance, Sean Wolf, William-EL (half), Neil Gibson, Brian Williams, Leslie Humphrey (my aunt who will always be loved) and all of the good men and women behind the wall with integrity.

I also appreciate those whom have adamantly ridiculed my initiatives. Your efforts have inspired me to ascend to higher heights………..

"KNOW THY SELF"

TABLE OF CONTENTS

WARNING!!!!

*The contents within this book are based on rare facts…

(READ AT YOUR OWN RISK)

INTRODUCTION

History has been so distorted throughout antiquity that people now seem to have a misconception of what actually took place in regards to human history. Some historians may be biased toward another nationality, which will often lead to the distortion and manipulation of facts in order to exalt one particular nationality over the other. I have assiduously researched and compiled historical data from various reliable sources, all of which I've concluded to be facts due to my own meticulous investigation. My research is unbiased, and although some may find the information within the contents of this book *mind blowing*, I definitely encourage you to do your own personal research so that you can come to your own conclusion as to what you find to be fact or fictitious. The Asian, European and African peoples of the world all have contributed much to the growth and development of the human race. This book's primary objective is to give you, the reader, unadulterated facts pertaining to certain historical events, peoples, cultures, and places so that they may have a clearer conception of the past in order to see through the illusion of misinformation that surrounds us in the present.

Our present day education system, unfortunately, only provides partial information when presenting historical data. I'm not speaking radical in any sense of the word about the United States' education system, nor am I suggesting that they change their present infrastructure. I will say that it's incumbent upon us as rational beings to logically assess the information taught to us and not always assume that the information presented is 100% accurate. In analyzing the standard American History books of the day, we can find an overwhelming hoard of information non-existent within the contents of these books. I will allow you to come to your own conclusion as to why this is so, but what I will do is share with you the missing history from which you rarely get to see or hear about.

"LET THERE BE LIGHT"

HISTORY'S MYSTERY

History only remains a mystery to those whom tarry upon desert sands hoping to find water instead of digging beneath the surface of dry land, which exist streams that flow abundant. This metaphor is to be taken both externally and internally, for if one wishes to begin the excursion in finding historical facts externally then he must internally dig away dry sands of any prejudices or bigotry that may reside so that his paradigm, like water, is crystal clear. How you perceive things is vital toward your research because the information you find can be mistakenly distorted if your paradigm is unclear. Your belief system gives birth to how you will perceive information received through your five senses. Most of us have been conditioned to have a prefixed view in regards to people, history and various cultures. This prefixed view is usually a creation of ignorant people whom have educated us with distorted history due to their own prejudices and/or lack of study.

"THE PERSON WHO UTILIZES THE FACULTIES OF THEIR MIND IS THE PERSON WHO WILL BE VICTORIOUS IN ALL OF LIFE'S ENDEAVORS"

Let us now reflect upon a story concerning the Chinese spy named Kim, who was scheduled to be executed for penalty of performing sorcery in public. As Kim sat in deep meditation within the confines of his cell awaiting his fate, he was suddenly interrupted by the eerie feeling of being watched. Kim looked up as he observed the huge silhouette of a guard on the opposite side of his cell. The guard insisted that Kim perform a magic trick of some sort before he was to be executed, and without hesitation Kim obliged.

Kim explained to the guard that before he proceeded he needed to inform him of something that was of great importance. The guard became curious as he knelt down to meet the intense gaze of Kim on the opposite side of the cell. Once Kim finished sharing the information with the guard, he immediately opened the cell door for Kim to escape. Kim was never to be seen again and the guard was later executed for neglect of duty. Kim was highly intelligent and people often mistook his ability to utilize reason and logic with him being some sort of sorcerer. Kim had convinced the guard that he was a member of a noble clan from which the guard had allegiance to. Without meticulous investigation or thorough questioning, the guard believed Kim's rhetoric, which inevitably led to his demise. As a spy, Kim was well informed on secret passwords, signs and traditional matters of noble clans, but if the guard only took a second to intelligently scrutinize Kim he may have been able to see past the illusion of Kim's strategic persuasion. In conclusion of this story, we can see that if one refuses to exercise their ability to rationalize and logically assess their circumference in this illusionary world then their neglect to do so will become their detriment.

"THE PERSON WHO UTILIZES THE FACULTIES OF THEIR MIND IS THE PERSON WHO WILL BE VICTORIOUS IN ALL OF LIFE'S ENDEAVORS."

THE MYSTERY OF HUMAN ORIGIN

There has been much controversy in regards to the origins of the human race. The bible is one of the world's most distributed books and is accepted by man as the standard authority pertaining to the creation of the human species. According to the bible God created man, who as to be the first human being on the face of the earth. Biblical scholars would concur that this particular event of human creation took place around 4500 B.C. Archeologists have uncovered human remains that have been carbon dated at several million years old, which is contrary to the biblical creation story of the first man. Charles Darwin's (1809-1882) theory of evolution explicated that man has only existed in his present physiological form no longer than 40,000 to 100,000 years. Modern human footprints have been found engraved in rock beneath the earth that was carbon tested at over 300 million years old, which predates the Jurassic era. Gold bracelets, necklaces and other jewelry were found beneath the earth in South Africa dating over 3.5 million years old. Tangible evidence of modern man's existence prior to the biblical story of creation and Charles Darwin's theory would compel an intelligent mind to meticulously scrutinize our present paradigm of human origins but to no avail, most of us remain sleep. There are various cultures through antiquity and today who adhere to the fact that human beings have been inhabiting the earth for hundreds of thousands of even millions of years. According to the Hindu Indian ideology, man not only exited on earth for millions of years but came to earth by way of highly advanced flying crafts called Vimana.

The Dogon tribe of West Africa proclaims that their vast knowledge of astronomy was passed down to them through their forefathers who themselves received this knowledge from a race of extraordinary beings that came from the Sirius star constellation. In Mesopotamia (Iraq), clay tablets were found possessing stories of man being the subject of a genetically altered species created by a superior raced of beings called the Anunaki. These Mesopotamian clay tablets were written in cunniform and are much older than the biblical story of creation. Ancient clay tablets, written by the Naacal priest were found in the old Rama Empire located in India. These old tablets described a civilization called "Mu," which existed over 50,000 years ago north of present day Hawaii, extending 5,000 miles from east to west and over 3,000 miles from north to south. The ancient ledgers of Egypt (KMT), Mexico, (Mayan Troano manuscript), Greece and Central America all mention the land of "Mu." The Naacal tablets also describe a creation story that strangely resembles the creative story of the bible, although the Naacal tablets predate the bible by thousands of years. Atlantis is another ancient civilization said to have existed on a continent between America and West Africa in the region known as the present day Atlantic Ocean. The Atlantean civilization that resided on this continent is speculated to have reached its golden age 100,000 years ago before its demise in 9564 B.C. The Pyramid city found 2,200 feet off the coast of Cuba is said to have been remnants of this lost civilization. The Greeks mention an ancient civilization located in the arctic region of the earth called Huberborea and Ultima Thule. A 4th century Greek navigator named Pytheas places this lost civilization in the region known presently as Greenland. An Indian intellectual named Bal Gangadhar Tilak (1856-1920) stated that the original home of humanity was in the arctic region of the earth and was destroyed between 10,000 – 8,000 B.C.

The ancient Lamas of Tibet were said to have known of an ancient underground civilization known as Agartha and Shambhala. According to the Lamas of Tibet, this Himalayan civilization of highly advanced humans possessed a profound knowledge of air travel, technology and lost spiritual secrets that would make modern cultures of the world look barbaric. The human citizens of this underground civilization are described to have harnessed the mysterious Vril force which was vehemently sought after b the Nazis in World War II. The mass accumulation of archeological findings alone would conclude that human being have in fact inhabited the earth for millions of years. There is one common factor that most religions and cultures of the world share when lecturing on the subject of human origin. This commonality is based upon the notion that humans are made up of living conscious energy or a soul that utilizes the physical body as a vehicle to co inhabit and interact with other dense molecular forms while on earth. It has been scientifically proven that when consciousness itself is focused on a particular point it profoundly affects the way subatomic particles react. This fact only substantiates the claim that the human being actually may be a soul or a living conscious energy being that our own consciousness can be directed to focus itself away from the physical body to effect the way subatomic particles react. Thus, one may conclude that the mystery of human origin is a study that journeys beyond the physiological composition of the body. "Who am I?" is a question often asked but rarely answered and if one would aspire to unlock the mystery that one must delve into the realm of fleshless things, traveling the vast dimensions of our own uncharted but dynamic minds.

THE HOLY BIBLE

The Holy Bible is translated as Helio Biblio in Latin, Helio-sun, Biblio-Book thus you have the book of the sun or the sol/soul. The majority of the stories in the bible are allegorical and based off of esoteric astrology. Jesus is the sun/son of God being born on December 25th. Astrologically December 21-25th is the winter solstice which brings in the birth of the sun because the length of days gets longer from this point. According to astrological science, the Virgo (September) is the only female sign of the Zodiac. It takes nine months for a woman to give birth to a child on average. If you were to count nine signs backwards starting with Leo, you will end your ninth count on the month of December. Thus you have a virgin birth! What about the story of Samson? He has seven locks which represent the rays of the sun. Delilah cut off Samson's locks When the sun travels around the Zodiac it enters into the month of September (Virgo) which is the autumn equinox. In this month, the sun loses its light and the length of days grows shorter. Thus we have the story of Samson (in brief). Jacob's twelve children represent the twelve tribes of Israel or the twelve signs of Zodiac. IS_RA_EL can be broken down into three parts. IS-Isis or moon, Ra—sun, El-star. We clearly have a clue who the children of Israel are, the children of the sun, moon and stars. Every human being was born under one of the twelve signs of the zodiac which make us all children of the twelve tribes of Israel in an esoteric sense. However, if we trace the actual historical lineage of Israel, we would find that the descendants of Israel are the dark-skinned, kinky-haired, thick-lipped people in American today. There were only two types of European people in the area at that time - Greeks and Romans. The Israelites were Hebrew; the original Hebrews were of Africoid stock. The present inhabitants of Israel today are only amalgamated relations between Africans (Hebrews/Canaanites) and Europeans (Romans/Greeks).

Christopher Columbus. On November 2 Columbus decided to send rodrigo de xerez and luis de torres, who had lived with the adelantado of murcia and was a jew and knew hebrew and Chaldaic and some Arabic to see the king of cuba, in order to present the letters and find out all that was necessary. Naturally, a man who knew Arabic, and another who knew the language of guinea, as we have heard before, were espeacially adapted to hold converse with the kings of the indies.

An interesting article from a book called the, 'Nero trailblazers", says Know ye that on the right side of the Indies there is an island called california, very near the terresrial paradise which is peopled by black women without any men among them, because they were acusyomed to live after the fashion of the Amozons. They were strong and hardy of bosies, of ardent courage and of great force. They had many ships in which they saied to other climes to carry out their forage to obtain booty. The various christian knights assembled to defend the Emperor of the Greeks and the city of constantinople against the attacks of the turks and the on this occasion the Queen of california and her court entered this war.

THE FALACY OF THE SLAVE TRADE. The trips from Africa to America took up to three to four months from east to west. According to history, these hundreds of Africans urinated on themselves during the journey. Four months of constant urination? These slaves would have drowned! Does this story make sense?????? If blacks were brought here tp North America around 1619 or even 1555, for that matter, than how were they taking slaves from newfoundland, to Europe? Keep in mind that one of the Native Americans even had the name , "ALI" and all were classified as Negro once they reached Valencia. How did a Native American in 1515 have a moorish name, "ALI"? the dogons were already on American land because they simply sailed over by way of world wide currents in the Atlantic. The first Africans to set foot on American soil were in fact the dogons of mali who used such currents as the canary and North equilateral current that recycles from West Africa to America and into the upper Atlantic ocean. This was before the invention of sails. The guinea current flows eastward along the guinea coast with frequent cycles out to sea where it joins the South Equatorial. The second group of Africans to land in the America were under the leadership of Abuakari in 1311 and had mixed in with the olmecs and became known as "Washo". At least 3,000 Americans are known to have been shipped to europe between 1493 and 1501 via the columbus expeditions, with the likely total being possibly double that. The tens of millions of Americans (so called indians) who dissappeared after 1492 did not all die in the holocaust inflicted within America, many thousands were sent to Europe and Africa as slaves. The whole slave trade myth is that the whole story was given to blacks in reverse. A mass colony of Africans were not shipped from Africa to America, but truth is that black indians were shipped from America to europe. They were then shipped from Spain to Africa as commodity for African resources. These black indians(now mistaken as Africans) were shipped back to America and classified as :African slaves". Africans and Native Americans by Jack D. Forbes/ Prince Hassan Bey/ Hakim bey- Moorish paradigm for references.

"A WISE MAN ONCE SAID THAT A TREE WITHOUT ROOTS CANNOT STAND"

1. The Aboriginal people of Australia have inhabited that continent for over 70,000 years.
2. Saint Nicholas or Santa Claus was a Greek bishop in the fourth century who was best known for his kindness.
3. The Indian population in the region of Hispaniola declined drastically when Columbus arrived in 1492 A.D. from 8 million to zero by 1535. This was due to the fact that the new explorers brought with them, germs that the Indians weren't familiar with.
4. The word "India" in the Latin language was derived from the Greek word "Indus" or "Indos," which means "Black."

5. Plato was one of the greatest minds of his time. He was a student of Egyptian philosophy.
6. Books are said to have been altered and deleted from the Bible at the Council of Nicaea 325 A.D.
7. Mizraim had offspring: Ludim, Anamim, Lehabim, Naphtuhim, Pathrusim and Casluhim; they were later to be attributed to the birth of the Philistines. (see Bible)
8. The Egyptians were descendants of Mizraim, son of Ham. Mizraim was considered to be the first "Egyptian." (see Bible)
9. A Jewish queen by the name of Dinah Cahens in the 7th century A.D. went to war and conquered an Arabian army. She had an army composed of Jews and Berbers, whom were victorious in their endeavors. Hakim bey- Moorish paradigm for reference.
10. The word "berber" is often used for the inhabitants of North Africa but is not an original African word. This is a derogatory term that means "barbarian" and was given to the people of that particular region by the Greeks and Romans.
11. The illustrious Moors, indigenous Africans, ruled Europe more than 700 years.
12. The Roman Empire was founded in the year 753 B.C. and ruled until 476 A.D.
13. In 65 B.C. the city of Jerusalem was captured by a brave Roman general named Pompey.
14. Hannibal, an African general of Cartherage, crossed the Alps on elephants with 26,000 of his warriors. Hannibal defeated the Roman armies for fifteen years in battle and some still refer to him as the father of military strategy. (218 B.C.)

15. Christopher Columbus, a great navigator, sailed the waters from 1492 - 1504. He discovered people of dark complexion on the islands close to the Americas.
16. Herodotus, a great Greek historian, was sincerely unbiased in his observation, study and research concerning peoples and cultures of the earth.
17. Ixliton was a Mexican god whose name meant black faced.
18. The Olmec tribe established civilizations in South and Central America before Christopher Columbus, the Indians, the Mayans or any other human beings. Until this day there still remain remnants of the great Olmecs, who were very industrious. The Olmec culture was very similar to that of Egyptian culture and it is said that they migrated from Africa's Nile Valley. Whether or not they did migrate from the East is not a fact, but from observation of the statutes, their facial features highly resemble African people.
19. Abu Bakr was the leader of the Almoravides, whom took over the city of Ghana in the year 1076 A.D.
20. The Phoenician-Canaanites spoke Hebrew and established a powerful metropolis in the 9th century B.C.
21. When the Empire of Mali was on the decline, the Songhay Empire began to flourish with the leadership of Sonni Ali in approximately 1350 A.D.
22. One of the earliest civilizations dates back to 4000 B.C.E. This civilization is known as the Mesopotamian Empire, established by the Sumerians. Sumerians were often called the "black headed people" (for reasons unknown).
23. The Moors, who ruled from 711 A.D. to 1492 A.D. in Europe, mastered the sciences of astrology, botany, mathematics, algebra (which derives from the

Arabic word "Al-jabrawal Muqubak"), chemistry, trigonometry, geometry, medicine, art and created the Arabic number system from 0-9, which we use to this very day.

24. Alexander the Great ruled Persia 332 B.C.E. Alexander was tutored by Aristotle, a highly respected philosopher of Greek origin.
25. Genghis Khan, a Mongol, created the largest empire on land in history.
26. American Indian names were also found amongst most Moors, whom inhabited Northwest Africa.
27. Christopher Columbus sent Rodrigo de Xeres and Luis de Torres to speak with the king of Cuba because the king spoke Arabic.
28. Among the Nanticoke Indians, who resided in Delaware as early as 1797, were men whom identified themselves as Moors.
29. Martin Luther was appointed to translate the Bible into German in the year 1525.
30. Napoleon Bonaparte (1769 - 1821) was the emperor of France in 1804 and was regarded as a powerful man of influence in his time.
31. Artifacts resembling Black people have been found in Peru, Panama, Columbia, Ecuador, Mexico and South America. These remnants date back from 2,000 B.C.E.
32. Constantine of the Roman Empire (330 A.D.) founded Constantinople and made it a recognized Christian city.
33. Buddhism, the religion, was founded by Siddhartha Guatama of India in the years between 563 - 483 B.C.E.

34. Mayan civilization was an offspring of the Olmec and began to develop in Central America around 1500 B.C.E.
35. Confucius, a Chinese philosopher, promoted good moral character and harmonious social order in the years between 551 - 479 B.C.E.
36. The founding fathers of the United States of America were very knowledgeable of the Native and Moorish American political system commonly known as the Iroquois League of Nations. They were so impressed that they decided to copy the format and employ it into the U.S. constitutional government.
37. The name "Osiris" means "Lord of the perfect black."
38. Shakespeare of Europe was very accomplished in his talent of drama and music around the time of 1564 -1616.
39. Albert Einstein, a brilliant scientist, baffled the world with his works on physics and mathematics. He also presented to the world the theory of relativity in 1916.
40. The British historian De Lacy O'Leary contended that most Greek and Roman scholars were born in Africa.
41. The great Indian savior and avatar Krishna lived 3000 years before Jesus, yet their stories are very similar. Krishna also means "The Black One."
42. Francois, a Roman Emperor, married Maria Theresa of Austria in the year 1735. Francois was also a member of a free Masonic order around this time.
43. In Sumter County, South Carolina, 1953, Ashton H. Williams, a Federal court judge acknowledged the fact that a black person, whom proclaimed his nationality to be "Moor," was not be classified as Negro, which at that time was a derogatory term that alluded to slavery, chattel and property.

44. The first nation to establish a treaty and recognize the United States' independence was Morocco.

45. Thales, Aristotle, Solon, Anaximander, Plato and Deocritus were Greeks' greatest masterminds.

46. Ancient Egyptians called or referred to themselves as Kam or Kam-Au, which means "Black-God" or "Black people." (see Egyptian language)

47. Herodotus, one of the world's most brilliant historians, referred to Egyptians as being a thick-lipped, broad nosed, wooly haired people with dark skin.

48. Galileo, a master astronomer, pointed out that there were moons around Jupiter.

49. Kamakura (1185 - 1313) of Japan was a chief who promoted martial arts philosophy to his samurai warriors.

50. Imhotep of Egypt is looked at as the father of medicine by most scholars and historians. He was an architect, high priest, poet, astrologer, physician, economist, diplomat, sage and magician.

51. The Dravidians, the original inhabitants of India, are now the least significant because of racial discrimination and India's caste system.

52. Francois Toussaint L'Ouverture was a leader of a revolt that rose up and went against slavery in Haiti.

53. Karl Marx (1818 - 1883) was a man best known for his socialist views based upon human perfectibility.

54. George Washington was chosen to be president of the United States in 1789. He was a great thinker of his time. George Washington also owned plenty slaves.

55. In 1804, Lewis and Clark were ordered by President Thomas Jefferson to navigate and explore the northwest region of the United States of America. They made sure to take with them Africans to watch over the food and clothing during the exploration. Upon their expedition they encountered an Indian tribe that had never seen Africans before and upon their approach the Indians began to worship and praise the Africans, because in their tradition at that particular time, to have dark skin was to be like that of the gods in heaven.
56. In 1881, Clara Barton founded the American Red Cross foundation, which has saved many lives.
57. Captain John Smith, in 1607, started the first English settlement in America in a region of the United States known as Virginia, Jamestown. His attempts to establish the colony were met with much opposition with the Indians through time, but eventually John Smith's mission prevailed.
58. Edgar Allen Poe, a poet of 1845, inspired literary work all over America.
59. Physical slavery was abolished as of December 6, 1865, pursuant to the 13th Amendment of the constitution. The bill explicated that physical slavery was only allowed if one were to be convicted of a crime.
60. Strabo (63 B.C.E. - 24 C.E.), a Greek geographer, concluded that the people known as Jews were closely connected to the Arabians and Egyptians.
61. The people commonly called Jews today are actually not the original Jews but a people known as Khazars. The Khazars merged into the culture of the original Jews and tactfully began to call themselves Jews around the time of 740 A.D. The Khazars did not descend from the house of Israel but came from Eastern Europe.

62. March 2, 1984, a *New York Times* editorial put forth that in Africa exists a tribe that has maintained their identity for over 2000 years and go by the name of the Falasha Jews from Ethiopia.
63. The United States declared war in May of 1846 with Mexico in what is now known as the Mexican War. Eventually about 12,000 U.S. troops took over the region known as Vera Cruz, which lead to the end of the war with the signing of a peace treaty on February 2, 1848.
64. Greek legends say that Egyptians and Phoenician conquerors initially ruled Greece up to the 14th and 15th century B.C.
65. Cheikh Anta Diop, a black historian, contributed many interesting views in regards to historical events of the past.
66. The founding fathers of the United States of America were Masons.
67. Certain historians contended that the present day Arab is a result of centuries long of amalgamation and intermarriage, which began in the 7th century.
68. Karl Marx said that the population and wealth of England, after slumbering for 700 years, began to develop itself under the influence of slave acquired capitol.
69. James I of England condemned all criminals to be deported to Virginia (1611 A.D.). Before that they were shipped to India.
70. Count Voley (1787 A.D.), a historian, said that Herodotus solved the problem of why the people of Egypt were so Negro in appearance, especially the Great Sphinx.

71. The enslavement of Africans didn't initially start as a racially motivated endeavor. In fact, Europeans were also used as slaves, but Africans were preferred over Europeans because of their strength to endure rigorous work loads.

72. Benjamin Banneker, a master astronomer, mathematician, scientist and architect, laid the blueprint for the construction of Washington D.C. He also published his own *Almanac* (1793) and was a crafty clockmaker. He also was a master mason.

73. William O. Bush (1845), the state senator in Washington, was awarded first prize for producing the world's finest wheat.

74. An Emperor of Morocco by the name of Mulai Ismael owned 10,000 European slaves. He used these slaves' toil to build stables in Mekne.

75. A king named Monomotapo, who held court in Zimbabwe, was very prestigious and wealthy. He owned plenty of gold and his empire extended 2,400 miles. He also ruled lower Ethiopia with a large military force full of not only men but fierce women at as his guard.

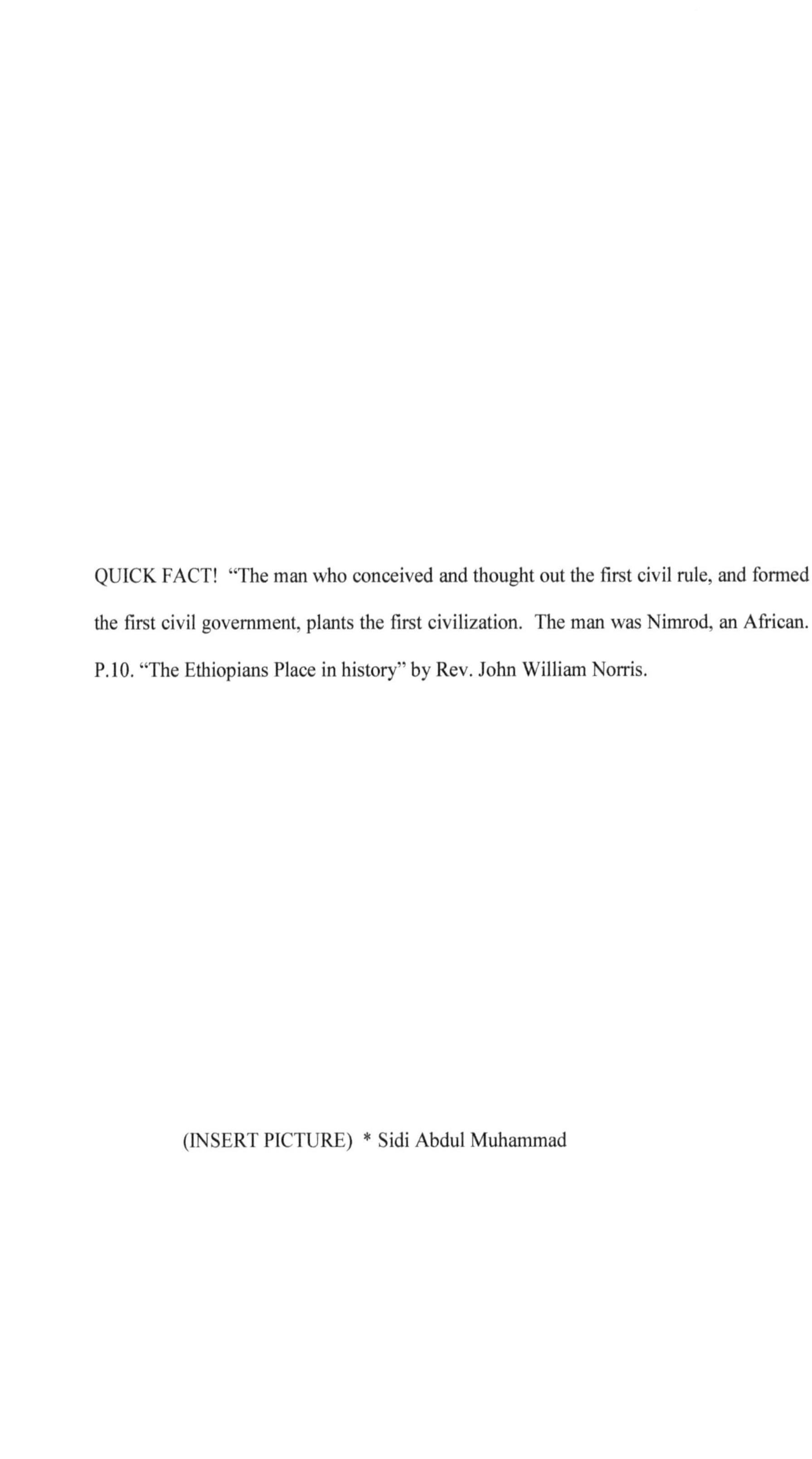

QUICK FACT! "The man who conceived and thought out the first civil rule, and formed the first civil government, plants the first civilization. The man was Nimrod, an African. P.10. "The Ethiopians Place in history" by Rev. John William Norris.

(INSERT PICTURE) * Sidi Abdul Muhammad

* Sidi Abdul Muhammad was a Moorish Emperor who signed the peace and friendship treaty with the United States, June 28 and July 15, 1786. Morocco was the first nation to recognize the United States' sovereignty and assisted them in establishing a government for themselves. George Washington wrote over 200 letters to the Emperor of Morocco and praised him for his clemency toward the United States.

76. There are pyramids in Mexico that are larger in volume than those in Egypt. There are also huge pyramids in China and Sudan that date back to 3000 B.C.
77. Certain entities of China mysteriously do not want anyone to take any pictures of or know about said pyramids, but the location and pictures of said pyramids can be found.
78. George Washington was once approached by a black man whom greeted him by tilting his hat and saying, "How do you do?" George Washington reciprocated by replying, "Fine, and you, sir?" Other Europeans who witnessed this were outraged and asked George Washington how he could greet a Negro as if he were a human being. George Washington said that the reason he returned the Negro's greeting was because he could never allow him to be more dignified then he was.

79. The Moors, original knights in shining armor, invented firearms, which were called fire sticks. They were called knights because the hue of their skin was very dark, like the night sky, but yet shiny due to the sweat that glazed their skin in the African heat.

80. Two thousand two hundred feet below, off the coast of Cuba, under the water, was found on ancient city with pyramids thought to be remnants of the mystical city of Atlantis.

81. The rulers of the Mali at the time of 1240 A.D. were Africans who were of the Mandingo Tribe.

82. The Queen of Sheeba was an Ethiopian Cushite queen also recognized as Makeda.

83. African born Septimus Severus, a Roman emperor, ruled Rome at the time of 193 A.D.

84. The city of Timbuctu was founded toward the end of the 11th century and gave birth to great kings such as the Inperial Mansa Kankan Musa.

85. Queen Charlotte Sophie was the grandmother of the great Queen Victoria. Queen Charlotte was a black mulatto woman.

86. Blind Tom was born about May 25, 1849. He was a pianist born blind but had an extraordinary ability. Blind Tom could hear a song one time and play back the exact song with absolutely no flaws.

87. In Mexico alone scientists say there are over 100,000 pyramids yet to be discovered. They came to this conclusion when analyzing pictures from a sky camera.

QUICK FACT! ....it is undoubtedly a fact that the Colchians are of Egyptian decent… My own idea on the subject was based on the fact that they have black skins and woolly hair (not that that amounts to much, as other nations have the same) and secondly, and more especially, on the fact that the colchians, the Egyptians, and the Ethiopians are the only races from which ancient times have practiced circumcision. Herodotus: The histories, penguin Books p. 167

88. Betovan was a student of Angelo Soloman, a Moor, whom taught Betovan masonry.
89. George Washington Carver broke down the molecular structure of plants by communicating with them in an unusual way. He also discovered a rare color of blue only known in Egypt.
90. The Olmec, who built the first civilization in America, also invented a complex calendar system on August 11, 3113 B.C., which the Mayans became accustomed to using. This calendar was projected to end December 21, 2012, which is the winter solstice.
91. The Chinese were skilled in navigation. Their historical ledgers show that they navigated to the Americas over thousands of years ago and described a people whom wore caps, sashes and had swords. These people were described as being dark-skinned. They had tigers, exotic birds and panthers, which were tamed. They called the Americas the country of refined gentlemen.
92. James Watt was inspired to invent a steam engine from watching the steam rise up from out of a tea kettle's spout (1769).

93. Portraits of a black Virgin Mary and baby Jesus exist in some churches throughout Europe.
94. Ceteway, Zulu king, defeated the British army and killed the Prince Napoleon.
95. Alexander the Greek or Great was a ruler who conquered most of the ancient world, extending his civilization east to India
96. A Zulu warrior could march 30-50 miles a day and still go into battle at the end of the day.
97. Horace Greely, a prominent businessman, owned the *New York Tribune*, which had a lot of influence on the minds of the American people at the time of 1850. The erroneous stereotypes of blacks being non-human and savage were promoted through this paper.
98. Marco Polo was an Italian explorer in the late 13th and early 14th centuries. He was best known for being one of the first Europeans to travel across Asia.
99. Horace Greely and Abraham Lincoln were both members of a political party, the Red Men Wig Party. This political name was switched to the White Men Wig Party.
100. The Adobe houses in Mexico are the same as the ones in North Africa. The opi Indian houses are the same as the Dogon in West Africa.
101. Hanno, a Carthaginian explorer (500 B.C.), traveled much of Africa's vast continent.
102. In the civil war there were Zoavay troops fighting from Algeria wearing fezes and they were known to be extremely vicious in battle.

103. Aesop (560 B.C.) was one of the world's greatest minds. He told fables and played upon the vanity of mankind with dexterity.

104. Greek philosophers such as Pythagoras (530 B.C.), Archimedes (287 - 212 B.C.), and Empedocles (430 B.C.) all have made magnificent contributions to the world with their philosophy and science.

105. Economic collapse and chaos were the result of the decline and fall of the Roman Republic 133 - 78 B.C.

106. Queen Cleopatra of Egypt, between 30 and 40 B.C., born three children; one by Caesar of Rome and twins by Mark Antony of Rome.

107. Queen Candace of Ethiopia (332 B.C.) was an empress, field commander and military tactician. Some say that Alexander the Great (upon his world conquering rampage) did not want to go beyond the borders of Ethiopia out of fear that if he was to be defeated by a queen and her army of excellent warriors, he would be humiliated. Whether this is true or fictitious, for whatever reason he did not want to penetrate into the borders of Ethiopia.

108. In 1795 the United States paid 1 million dollars to the Algerian pirates that held 115 seamen in September of 1795. The United States continued to pay annual tributes.

109. Oliver Crowell, a black man, crossed the Delaware with George Washington on December 26, 1776. This was a man that George Washington thought of highly. So highly that he wrote out his discharge papers personally from his own hand.

110. The first Punic war in Rome, Italy, began about 260 B.C. The population at the time was estimated to be around 4 million, which was the same as Macedonia's

population. In this same time period, Egypt's population was about 10 million and Syria's approximately 30 million.

111. Spartacus, of the first century B.C., was a Roman slave who defeated many Roman armies.

112. Prince Wipple's identity has been suppressed because he was a black man that taught George Washington esoteric sciences. Prince Whipple passed November 18, 1796, and was buried in North Cemetery, Portsmouth New Hampshire.

113. The Barbary pirates of Algiers, Tunis and Tripoli roamed the seas capturing vessels, holding men for ransom and often patrolled the western end of the Mediterranean, which nations such as Britain and the United States did trade. These Barbary pirates collected taxes from the United States and Britain.

114. The "War of the Roses" was a term that stemmed from the late 15th century battle between the English families. This war was for rule of the country and it consisted of the House of York, who had an emblem of a white rose, and the House of Lancaster, who had a red rose as their emblem. Eventually the House of Lancaster won the battle.

115. Amina was a warrior Queen of Zazzua, a province of Nigeria now known as Zaria. She was best known for her military skill and the fact that she built a defensive wall around her military camps. As time went on, towns began to develop within these defensive walls that still exist to this day. Those walls are known as ganuwar Amina or Amina's walls.

116. The seven wonders of the ancient world are: the Pyramids of Egypt, the Statue of Zeus by Phidias, the Colossus of Rhodes, the Temple Artemis at Ephesus, the

Hanging Gardens of Babylon, the Mausoleum at Halicarnassus and the Lighthouse of Alexandria. The only wonder that hasn't disappeared is the pyramids of Egypt.

117. Prince Albert was a 9th century German prince that married Queen Victoria of Britain and died in his early forties. As a result of his death, Queen Victoria mourned him until she subsequently died.

118. Makeda (960 B.C.) ruled Ethiopia, a region known as Nubia Kush Axum and Sheba. Ethiopia was ruled by a lineage of Nubian queens one thousand years before Jesus Christ's birth. At that time, Ethiopia was an extremely powerful nation. Next to Egypt, Ethiopia was the wealthiest and most prosperous kingdom in the world.

119. Jesse James was an outlaw who robbed banks and trains in the 1870's. Jesse James was eventually shot in the back by one of his own men for promise of a reward.

120. Immanuel Kant, an 18th century German philosopher, was known for his three philosophical works: *Critique of Pure Reason, Critique of Practical Reason* and *Critique of Judgment.* Immanuel Kant's philosophy was that we cannot know a thing in itself as it is, but only as our mind constitutes it.

121. Nzingha was an Amazon queen of West Africa Angola (1582 - 1663). Nzingha was a powerful warrior queen who went to war with the Europeans trying to penetrate into Africa. Portuguese slave traders were insistent upon capturing Africans and making them into slaves, but the Angolan Amazon queen would not conform or allow it by any means. Nzingha waged war against European slave

hunters for more than thirty years, making it extremely hard for European forces to accomplish their objectives. Her inevitable death on December 17, 1663, opened the way for the Portuguese to conquer the people and acquire slaves.

122. A French philosopher in the 17th century named Rene Descartes stated that he had found that it was impossible for him to doubt that he existed since he himself was doing the doubting in the first place. He was best known for his philosophical phrase: "I think therefore I am."

123. In the year 1492 the Moorish empire in a region known as Grenada, Spain, was conquered by the armies of King Fernand and Queen Isabella. This marked the beginning of Spanish European domination in that particular region. The Christians ran Spain and it was the end of a more than 700 year rule of Islamic Moorish ideology.

124. Protagoras, a Greek philosopher, is best known for his statement: "Man is the measure of all things."

125. Sitting Bull is the name of the Native American chief from the Sioux tribe. Sitting Bull was not only a chief but a medicine man and warrior who fought against the settlers in the Northern Great Plains.

126. A German alchemist, Johann Bottger (1707), discovered the famous Meissen porcelain works.

127. General George Patton was a general in World War II. He was best known for his leadership and expertise in warfare using tanks and other war vehicles.

128. Behanzin Hossu Bowelle (the King Shark) 1841 - 1906 was a 9th century West African ruler. The Europeans tried to enter into his country but the King Shark's

army of female warriors smashed the Europeans upon their attempts. Behanzin was also very talented in poetry and music.

129. Leo Africanus, an Islamic Moor, converted to the Jewish faith. He stated that the Jews of North Africa were not original but hybrids. They were a mixture of intermarriage amongst the Greeks, Spaniards, Portuguese, vandals and Romans.

130. When Captain Cook arrived in Hawaii 1779, he and his crew brought with them syphilis, tuberculosis, influenza and gonorrhea. The decline of Hawaii's population was drastic, dropping from 500,000 to 84,000 in 1853.

131. The oldest record of martial arts techniques were found in Egypt (for a point of reference see *African Presence in Early Asia* by Van Sertima/Rashidi).

132. Some historians say that the original name of Africa was Akibalon. The change came when Roman General Scipio Africanus defeated the General Hannibal, which resulted in naming the continent that was formally known as Akibalon after Scipio Africanus in honor of him.

133. The Shang dynasty (1500 - 1000 B.C.) of China established the basics of calligraphy that still exist to this day. China's first emperor was Fu-His (2953 - 2838 B.C.), a black man. The Shang was given the name Nakhi, which if broken down into English is Na-Black and Khi which means "man."

134. The Dogon tribe of West Africa Mali could draw and explain accurately the positions of the celestial bodies in the skies without using any modern technology. Scientists are perplexed at the Dogons, whom told of the composition of the moon in the year 1946 before anyone even went to the moon. The Dogon had been saying for years that there was a white dwarf star, Sirius B, which was invisible.

Recently scientists found what the Dogon had said about the particular star were true. When scientists asked how they knew so much about the celestial bodies without the usage of technology, they replied by pointing into the sky in the direction of Sirius constellation and said, "Extraterrestrials."

135. Colonel William Byrd wrote Lord Egnont a letter dated July 12, 1736, stating that, "The presence of Aethiopians amongst them would blow up the pride and ruin the industry of poor white people who seeing a rank of poor creatures below them detested work for fear it should make them look like slaves. It's a shame to know that people account it more like gentle men to steal then to dirty their hands with labor of any kind."

136. Nikola Tesla (1856 - 1943), a scientist, invented electrical devices including a.c. dynamos, transformers, and motors. He also invented free energy devices, anti-gravity airships and radar technology that can be used as a death ray weapon.

137. James Watt, a mechanical engineer, invented the modern steam engine (1765).

138. Prince Hall (1735 - 1807) served in the American Revolutionary War and also became the founder of Black Freemasonry.

139. Some modern inventions by blacks include: traffic lights, toilets, the multiple stage rocket, air conditioning, automatic transmission and firearms.

140. Harriet Beecher Stowe, Count Adam Gurowski, Henry Longfellow, Ralph Waldo Emerson, John Adam, Thomas W. Higginson, Benjamin Lundy, Charles Summer, Joshua Ciddings, Wendel Phillips, Gerit Smith, John Quincy Adams, John Greenleaf Whittier, Henry Ward Beecher and William Lloyd Garrison were Europeans who were in total opposition to the ideal of slavery.

141. Susan B. Anthony (1820 - 1906) was a leader in that she opposed slavery at a time when its ideology was most prevalent.

142. On January 8, 1886, a man by the name of Timothy Drew was born. Later to be known as Noble Drew Ali, this great mind contributed to the upliftment of the black people in North America by teaching them the science and knowledge of themselves in order to get them out of the ignorant state of mind that they were in from centuries of being slaves in America. Noble Drew Ali founded the Moorish Science Temple of America, where he taught the words "Negro," "Black," "colored" and "Ethiopia" were derogatory terms placed upon people of hue in order to trick them out of their nationality and place them in the folds of property, chattel or slaves. By proclaiming their nationality they would be recognized by the government and the nations of the earth as a free Moorish national and entitled to all the rights and privileges of a human being on the shores of America. In 1929 Noble Drew Ali passed, and the stock market crashed, which was the beginning of the great depression.

143. The Mexican War started when James K. Polk, the President, ordered General Zachary Taylor to seize disputed Texan land that was settled by Mexicans. The United States declared war on May 13, 1846.

144. In the year of 1826, Thomas Jefferson and John Quincy Adams passed away on July 4.

145. The first Continental Congress was held in Philadelphia on September 5 and October 26, 1774, calling for civil disobedience against the British.

146. The late, great Captain William Kidd was arrested, sent to England and hanged for violation of piracy in the year of 1701.

147. The oldest president of the United States to leave office was Ronald Regan at the age of 77.

148. Heraclitus (540 - 475 B.C.E.) and Zeno (335 - 263 B.C.E.) were great Greek philosophers that contributed a lot toward the development of the Greek era.

149. The Netherlands (Holland) begot William Frederick, the prince of Orange. He led a revolt against the French rule in the year of 1813 and was later crowned king in 1815.

150. Ulysses Simpson Grant, a Republican, was the 18th president of the United States of America. He also fought in the Mexican War.

151. In 1921 the Klu Klux Klan began to bring violence upon the Catholics in the North, South and Midwest.

152. A man by the name of Booker T. Washington founded the Tuskegee Institute for blacks (1881).

153. In the year of 1814 the British landed in the state of Maryland and defeated the United States' forces and burned down the Capitol and the White House.

154. In the year of 1731 Benjamin Franklin founded the first American circulating library in Philadelphia.

155. The great King Taharka of Nubia (710 - 664 B.C.) was the ruler of not only Cush or Ethiopia but Egypt as well by the age of 32. Takarka is responsible for building the temple at Gebel Barkal in Sudan, which had rock carved into the image of

himself at 100 feet high. This great king is also mentioned in the bible (Isaiah 37:9; 2 Kings 19:9).

156. Sir Francis Bacon in the year of 1697 published *The Essays*, which became a best-seller. Sir Francis Bacon was a master in the esoteric sciences and studied as well as traveled in Fez Morocco, Egypt and Spain.

157. Thutmose III was the pharaoh of Egypt (1504 - 1450 B.C.) and came from one of the greatest royal families in the world. He extended the rulership of ancient Egypt all the way into western Asia.

158. Tenkamenin was the king of Ghana (1037 - 1075) and was known for being a very gregarious king in regards to the well-being of his people. He would get on his horse and ride around listening to the concerns of his people each day. Tenkamenin's greatest strength was governmental structure and policies.

159. On October 12, 1492, Christopher Columbus and his crew sighted land, which came to be the present day Bahamas. He also discovered that there were people already there whom looked as they were Ethiopian or Moorish in origin.

160. In 1807 a man by the name of Robert Fulton made the first practical steam boat trip.

161. Tiye, the Nubian queen of Egypt (1415 - 1340 B.C.), was regarded as one of the most beautiful queens in Egyptian history. For nearly a half a century Tiye governed the affairs of Egypt or Kemet. She was believed to be the standard of beauty in the ancient world.

162. The longest serving president alive is General Gnassingbe Eyadema of Toga, who became president on April 14, 1967.

163. King Khufu of ancient Egypt or Kemet (2551 - 2528 B.C.) was the father of pyramid building. In Greece they call him Cheops and he is responsible for building the great pyramids of Giza.

164. The earliest use of the wheel for transportation purposes goes back 5,500 years ago to ancient Mesopotamia, present day Iraq.

165. Menelek II was king of kings in Abyssinia (1844 - 1913). Menelek II was responsible for uniting the kingdoms of the United States and Ethiopia.

166. Charles Jenen, of the United States, from 1954 to 1994 had a whopping 970 operations to remove his tumors.

167. The earliest canal was found in Mandali, Iraq, which dates back to 4,000 B.C.

168. The oldest woman who ever lived was Jeanne Louise of France. She lived to be 122 years old. (February 21, 1875 - August 4, 1997)

169. Narmer was the founder of Dynastic Kemet or Egypt (3200 B.C.). He was the leader of the army of upper Kemet, which was located in the south to conquer lower Kemet that existed in the north around 3200 B.C. After he accomplished his mission he united the two regions as one. 30 Dynasties followed Narmer's rulership. The city of Memphis was named Men-Nefer by the Greeks and to this day that name still honors this African king who lived 5,000 years ago.

170. Valentina Teresh Kova from U.S.S.R. was the first woman ever to launch into space.

171. The oldest human footprints were found in Laetoli, which is northern Tanzania. They date back to 3.6 million years ago.

172. Queen Victoria was the longest reigning queen. She ruled for 63 years as Queen of Britain and the Empress of India.

173. The world population in 1955 was 2.56 billion and as of 2005 it was over 6 billion.

174. Osei Tutu was the king of Asante in West Africa Ghana (1680 - 1717). He amazingly united six nations under his rule and leadership.

175. Benito Mussolini, an Italian general, formed a fascist government in Italy and allied forces with Germany in the 1920's.

176. Samory Toure was the king of Sudan (1830 - 1900). King Samory Toure was a military tactician who united West African forces in order to fight against the French, whom were at the time trying to exploit Africa.

177. The oldest mummy dates back to the 4th dynasty of the Egyptian pharaohs (2600 B.C.).

178. Yahya Jammeh is the youngest current head of state. He was born 1965 and became elected president on September 27, 1996.

179. Li Po (705 - 762), a Chinese poet, expressed his poetry in such a way that most people report feeling it in their soul upon reading his material.

180. Richard Strauss (1864 - 1949) was a German composer. He was best known for his extraordinary composing abilities.

181. The Sanskrit Hindu book *Mahabharata* consists of 18 books and 90,000 stanzas. It was put together around 300 B.C.

182. Senworsert I was the pharaoh of ancient Egypt/Kemet in the 12th dynasty (1897 B.C.). He was such an extraordinary king that the Greeks honored him dearly.

183. Adolf Hitler was a German leader in the 20th century. He led the Nazi party and was also responsible for the murders of six million Jews. His objective was to create a pure race of white people to rule the world. Hitler and the Nazi party fought in World War II but were defeated.

184. Aquinag Thomas (1225 - 1274) was a theologian from Italy whose works formed the basis of the Roman Catholic Church theology.

185. Shaka was the king of the Zulus (1818 - 1828). He was a genius military strategist who developed the "assegai," a short stabbing spear. Shaka Zulu built a nation of Zulus over a million strong. When their enemies would see them they would sometimes flee at the sight of them because of the fierce reputation as a mighty people. At the time when the Europeans were trying to colonize, Shaka united all of the ethnic groups of South Africa to drive them away.

QUICK FACT! …a great many of the most distinctive practices of Egyptian civilization suddenly appeared in more distant parts of the coastlines of Africa, Europe, and Asia, and also in course of time in Oceania and America; and to suggest that the Phoenicians must have been the chief agents in initiating the wholesale distribution of this culture abroad….. Lecture delivered in the John rylands Libarry, by Elliot smith.

(

186. Adolf Eichmann was a Nazi official responsible for the killing of many Jews around the time of the Holocaust.

187. The Rothchild family started building their wealth in the 18th century. They are a family of European bankers. Throughout history they have financed the British as well as the French emperor Napoleon Bonaparte.

188. W.E.B. DuBois was a radical thinker and black author in the late nineteenth century and early twentieth century. Late in his life he decided to join the American Communist Party.

189. The Ku Klux Klan is a secret society that promotes white supremacy. This organization began in the south at the time of the reconstruction and they were opposed to blacks being able to have equal rights as citizens. They maimed, hanged and killed blacks and attacked Jews, communists and Roman Catholics. The Ku Klux Klan or KKK wear white hoods and have titles such as Grand Cyclops and Inperial Wizard.

190. The world's oldest known alphabet was found on clay tablets. There were 32 wedge shaped letters in cuneiform style on the tablets. They were found in Syria and date back to 1450 B.C.

191. The United States Army Corps is the largest air force in world history.

192. The oldest tree that still grows on the earth to this day is the Maidenhair or the Ginko Biloba tree, which is from China. Its kind is 160 million years old.

193. A man by the name of Andreas Mihavecz of Austria went a mind blowing 18 days without food or water at the age of 18 from April 1, 1979 to April 18, 1979.

194. Neil Armstrong was an astronaut from the United States. He was the first man to set foot on the moon, July 20, 1969. There were allegations of this particular moon landing to be false and an illusion put out to the masses.

195. One out of every nineteen people in North Korea was a member of their military in the year 1999.

196. Sir Francis Drake of the 16th century was the first English navigator to sail around the world.

197. Paul Signac (1863 - 1935) was a French artist known for his elaborately painted mosaic like blocks and beautiful landscapes.

198. Cordovero Moses (1522 - 1570) was a Palestinian Jewish mystic who was best known for his Kabalistic teachings.

199. Ramses II of ancient Kemet or Egypt was one of the greatest builders in Egyptian history. He is attributed to the buildings of Abu Simbel, Karnak and the Luxor temples. He added to and contributed many more statues as well as a statue of himself at Ramesseum.

200. Moor was a title used to refer to the blacks of the Moorish empire, which was Northwestern and Southwestern Africa extending across the great Atlantic unto present day North, South and Central America.

201. Around the time of 1322 - 1465 the Catholic Spanish authorities stopped the Moors from practicing masonry, ceramic, shipbuilding, medicine and tailoring.

202. The *Newsweek* magazine dated January 11, 1988, depicts a black Adam and Eve on the front of the headline. This article said that everyone that exists today descended from an African woman who they call Eve 200,000 years ago.

203. April 30, 711, General Tarik arrived on the Spanish coast with 7,000 troops. There were 300 Arabs and 6,700 native Africans called Moors.

204. One king of Moorish Spain owned 600,000 books in his personal library because of his insatiable lust for knowledge. The city of Cordova had 800 public schools alone.

205. Moorish architectural structures still remain in Seville, Cordoba, and Grenada, Spain today.

206. The Smithsonian put out a text called *The Native Americans* (1991). The Osage and Arikara of the southeast plains are described as wearing head coverings called turbans.

207. During the reign of Hisham II (976 - 1009 C.E.), a Muslim navigator, Ibn Farrukh of Grenada, Spain, sailed from Kadesh (February 999 C.E.) in the Atlantic Ocean and landed in the Canary Islands visiting King Cuaraiga. He continued to sail toward the west and observed two islands, Capraria and Pluitana.

208. Colonel Braghine said he saw a collection in Ecuador consisting of a statuette of a black man who was 20,000 years old.

209. Peter Marty, a friend of Christopher Columbus and a historian, said he saw aboriginals Negros in Panama in 1513.

210. The Romans entered the west region of Africa in 46 B.C. They saw Africans that were black and called them "Marues," from which the word "Moor" is derived from. The lands of Mauritania and Morocco were derivations of the name Moor indigenous to that particular region.

211. Moors ruled the British Isles over 500 years after the Romans rule and previously to the rule of the Normans in 1066.

212. The great pyramid is located directly in the center of the earth's land mass.

213. March 17, 1490 - 1492 was the time that the Moors were lost their stronghold in Ireland, Spain, England and Northwest Africa.

214. According to the *Cambridge Encyclopedia,* the Mexican Messiah "Quetzalcoatl" was a black wooly-haired god.

215. Billy Simmons, an African Jew of the 1850's, said he was from the tribe of the Israelites named Recabites. He was originally from Madagascar and lived in the Northwest region of Africa. Top Jewish authorities never questioned or doubted his claims.

216. Statutes of Indian gods located in Central America possess black features that irrefutably represent those people of African decent.

217. Peter Martyr, a historian and friend of Christopher Columbus, spoke of Africans that lived in Central America. He said these were the first Africans seen in the Indies.

218. Christopher Columbus' personal journal of the third voyage states that he wanted to find out what the Indians of Hispaniola had told him that there had come from the south and southeast Negro peoples who brought those spear points made of a metal which they call guanim (p. 6).

219. Legally the word "Moor" was only a title used to refer to those persons whose ancestry or allegiance was linked in some way to the dominions of Amexem or the Moorish Empire.

220. Outside of Ireland there exists a little island called Achill Beg or Achill Bey as it was named and pronounced by the Moors whom inhabited the island around the time of 1200 to 1400 A.D.

221. Christopher Columbus said that upon encountering the native people of the Caribbean he recognized or presumed their language to be Arabic.

222. The *Science* magazine dated September 11, 1987, said that Africa was the cradle of modern humans.

223. A Muslim navigator, Hhashkhash Ibn Saeed Ibn Aswad of Cordoba, Spain, sailed from Palos in 889 C.E., crossed the Atlantic, reached an unknown territory (Ard Majhoola) and returned with fabulous treasures. The unknown territory is known as present day America.

224. The clothes of Peruvian women resemble the same style as that of Moorish women.

225. Roman Emperor Caligula (12 - 41 C.E.) had a law that insisted that bathing was a crime.

226. Anastsius I (430 - 518 C.E.) was the emperor of Byzantium. The enlightened men and high priest warned him that he would one day be killed by lightning. This made him very paranoid and often lead him to overreact when lightning struck by running for shelter. To his demise, he ran for cover in an old house one day when lightning struck and the ceiling of the old house fell down on him and killed him.

227. Empress Tz'u-hsi of China (1835-1908) ate 2 million dollars worth of pearls over a time period of about 47 years with the assumption that the pearls would give her a vibrant, youthful glowing look.

228. R.E. McMaster Jr., author of *The Power of Total Perspective,* said that there are two views of history: (1) History happens by chance and coincidence or accident. (2) It is planned. The general public is taught that history happens by chance and accident, however, the upper echelon knows that history is planned.

229. John Hanson (1721 - 1783), a black man, was the first President of the United States. Strangely, there are a variety of different images of John Hanson. Some of them seem to resemble a European man, some resemble a mulatto man and a few still uphold the original image of John Hanson.

230. The United States government was incorporated on February 21, 1871.

231. The Greeks originally gave the Ethiopians the word "Ethiopian" because it meant burnt or black face. Those people called themselves "Abyssinians."

232. The Portuguese were major slave traders and were the first Europeans to trade on the west coast of Africa.

233. When archaeologists dug up skeletal remains found in the mound pyramids in several locations, they made a most astonishing find. The remains were all seven to eight feet in height.

234. The location of the United States is in the District of Colombia according to the laws of the Uniform Commercial Code 9-307(h). Also Article I Sec. 8, Clause 17 of the U.S. Constitution.

235. In Carl H. Claudy's book, *Masonic Harvest*, he writes of an elaborately defined utopia on earth that was in dire need, due to the present state of society on earth. The new utopia would leave all men, women and children blissful, happy and content.

236. Al Gore once said that God was within. He said that God was not some personal being somewhere "out there" in a place called heaven. Every man is God, every man has God within. Al Gore is the author of *Earth the Balance and Ecology and the Human Spirit.*

237. Newt Gingrich, former speaker of the House of Representatives, is said to be a mason. He was once photographed standing next to a young man wearing a t-shirt that said, "Ordo Ab Chao," which is a Latin phrase meaning "order out of chaos." This is a known motto for masonry.

238. The Aztec calendar stone was found in 1760. It's 12 feet wide, weight over 20 tons. The Aztecs possessed knowledge of astrology that was handed down to them through the Olmec civilization, whom inhabited the land previously.

239. President Harry Truman (1884 - 1972) was uneducated, but from an early age until the age of 14 he took the initiative to educate himself by reading every book in the Independence Missouri library.

240. In the 1960's people began to say that there was an overpopulation problem on the earth when there was absolutely no scientific evidence to support the erroneous claim. Organizations such as Zero Population Growth and National Organization for Women were founded in an attempt to propagate the erroneous claims.

241. President Ronald Reagan once wrote a letter to Fred Kleinknecht, Sovereign Grand Commander. He was honored to join the ranks of sixteen former presidents in their association with Freemasonry. (*The New World Order* by Ralph Epperson)

242. In the 18th century Europe, the people at the time thought that if they took a bath they would get sick. As a result, no one bathed, which caused many diseases, foul odor in the air and death. Queen Victoria herself once fainted as a result of this dilemma while sailing on a yacht in the Thames River in England.

243. A man by the name of Edwin Booth saved the life of Abraham Lincoln's son, Robert Todd Lincoln (1843 - 1926). Edwin Booth was John Booth's brother, whom later killed Abraham Lincoln.

244. It is said that the real reason for World War II was to establish a centralized global police force, which is the present day United Nations; second to make Germany completely subjugated and dependent commercially.

245. The dejure forum of government is represented by the constitutional republic (1787), Constitution of the United States of America. The defacto forum of government is represented by or as a legislative democracy (1871), Constitution of the "UNITED STATED."

246. The Amendatory Act of March 9, 1933, declared every citizen of the United States an enemy of the government.

247. Alexander the Great died at the ripe age of 32 because of intoxication and self inflicted debauchery which debilitated his body.

248. The Portuguese arrived in Sierra Leone in 1462, Guinea around 1446 and the Canary Islands in the year of 1341.

249. Thomas Fuller (1710 - 1790), a black mastermind, was called by people of his time the African Calculator. He was a mathematical genius who could figure out equations in his head without having to write it out on paper. Brissot de Warville, who was from France, once asked him how many seconds in a year and a half and he quickly replied, "4,904,000."

250. Some of the first slaves in the United States were white European English men. Both Europeans and Africans were slaves. Europeans were often sold into slavery as far as Africa.

251. George Downing (1819 - 1903), a New York caterer, was so skilled in his craft that he was asked to take over the restaurant of the House of Representatives.

252. The Romans got their culture from Greeks, whom were civilized and taught by ancient Kemetins or Egyptians.

(

253. Scipio Africanus conquered Hannibal and married a young lady by the name of Aemilia.

254. President George Washington's bodyguard, Thomas Hickey, was an agent from the British sent to kill George Washington. Phoebe, a black woman, was Washington's housekeeper at the time and learned of Hickey's secret plot to kill the President. Hickey had poisoned a dish of peas that was to be served to

Washington. Just as Washington was about to eat the peas, Phoebe stopped the President. George Washington then threw the peas out of the window to some chickens that ate them and died. Thomas Hickey was executed on June 28, 1776.

255. Pompey led an army of Roman soldiers to the Golden Fleece of Prometheus and made war with the Iberians. The Amazon women at this time inhabited a portion of the land. Although the Amazon women assisted the Iberians in the war with the Roman soldiers, they could not find one Amazon corpse on the battlefield after the war.

256. December 1, 1862, in the annual message, President Lincoln said, "In a certain sense the liberation of slaves is the destruction of property----property acquired by descent or by purchase the same as any other property."

QUICK FACT!. Wihelm Reich born 1897 Austrian-American created the Orgon Accumulator. This was a device that could strengthen the immune system, cure ailments and eliminate cancerous tumors on the body. Reichs ideology was that there was a certain type of energy that existed everywhere from which he called , "Orgone'. Through reichs portable devices he could cure certain human ailments and would later construct other machines that would extract this free energy to manipulate weather conditions, also Reich invented a machine that would provide health, free energy and weather stability to humanity. Feb, 10 1954 reichs was under fire from the FDA. June 5 1956, the FDA destroyed Reichs orgon Accummulators and in later months, all of his papers & books. The following year reich was sent to federal prison eventually dying in his sleep from supposed heart failure . Tesla also invented technology that would aoffer free-energy to humanity. After his death, all of his property, books, notes and papers were seized by the FBI. Thomas Henry Moray was yet another fantastic inventor who created an energy device which he called the solid state detector. His machine was later termed the "Moray Valve" and attracted the attention of the mainstream media along with other Corporations such as bell Labortories. Morays device could extract radiant energy that was free and unlimited in the atmosphere.

*

257. September 13, 1862, President Lincoln said that the American people didn't go to the war to put down slavery but to put the flag back.

258. Charles VII (1422 - 1461), the French king, used African physicians because of their expertise and accomplished minds.

259. Alice was a slave born in 1686 on the island of Barbados. Many looked up to her because of her wisdom. She lived for 116 years.

260. President Gerald Rudolph Ford, an All-American football star, was offered a contract to play with the Green Bay Packers and the Detroit Lions but chose to go to law school instead.

261. In 610 B.C., the Egyptians built a canal that connected the Mediterranean via the Nile and Red Sea.

262. James Forten (1776 - 1842) was a rich, black man in an era when slavery was prevalent. He was a sail manufacturer and was a relevant figure in the anti-slavery movement.

263. The elder Seneca (55 B.C. - 41 A.D.), a writer, gave a clear conception on the subject of Agustian schools of thought.

264. Benjamin Franklin was a member of the Philadelphia Lodge of Freemasonry in 1732 and was the Grand Master by 1734.

265. The banking system can create money and credit which gives them power over the governments that create policy.

266. Karl Marx, the founder of the communist ideology, is looked upon by many as a great mind of his time. His best friend, Fredrick Engels, was a very wealthy man. Karl Marx detested capitalism, yet he leached money off of his friend, whom acquired his money through the ideals of capitalism. Karl Marx only worked as a

newspaper correspondent for a short period of time, which was the only job he had his whole life.

267. Karl Marx was a member of a satanic church and he detested the ideology of Christianity and the Jews.

268. Karl Marx committed adultery in a defiant act to prove his disdain toward traditional family values.

269. Karl Marx allowed two of his children to starve to death in a defiant act to prove his disdain toward traditional family values.

270. Norman Dodd, the director of the committee to investigate tax exempt foundations/House of Representatives, said that the trustees of the particular foundation asked if there were any other means to alter a mass of people's lives other than war. Upon contemplating the thought for an entire year, they came to the conclusion that it wasn't. It resulted in the question of how they could get the United States involved in a war in order to alter the lives of the American people.

271. Some people feel that World War I began when Archduke Francis Ferdinand was assassinated June 28, 1914.

272. World War I was preplanned five years prior to the actual war in an attempt to alter the lives of the people.

273. America's initial position in World War I was neutral but the hidden powers were planning to secretly involve America by sinking the Lusitania.

274. The American ship Lusitania was destroyed along with the lives of 1201 people on board, but surprisingly this act did not prompt President Woodrow Wilson to declare war against Germany.

275. The hidden agenda behind bringing the war about was to create a world government or new world order, which started with the League of Nations.

276. President Woodrow Wilson was a given a declaration of war from Congress on April 2, 1917, which allowed the U.S. to enter the war with the excuse that they were trying to make the world a better and safer place for democracy.

277. The League of Nations charter was ratified January 10, 1920, but was not accepted by the Senate when presented by Woodrow Wilson because of the American people's suspicions with getting involved with the affairs of and permanently creating alliances with foreign countries.

278. After the worldwide cataclysm in 1500 B.C., the Moabites, Canaanites, Hittites and Amorites received permission from pharaohs of Egypt to settle in the North and Southwest region of Africa, which eventually sprouted the Moroccan Empire.

279. According to the ancient Arabian records, the Tamu people were the oldest and the first people of Arabia. According to the *Encyclopedia of Islam 1911*, the Tamu people were the Amalakites. Historically, the Amalakites are from the seed of Ham.

280. The Yuroba and the Ashanti people say that their ancestors came from the eastern end of Africa. This confirms that the ancient Canaanite, Amorite, Hitite peoples migrated from the east to west end of Africa after 1500 B.C.

281. World War II was a war designed by the powerful elite in order to bring about a new world government, which we commonly call the United Nations.

282. A deadly chemical called Zyklon 8 was used in Germany's concentration camps to kill Jews. This lethal gas was manufactured by the business I.G. Farben, which American bankers created.

283. (1945) Japan wanted to end the war with the United States. The U.S. didn't want to end the war because some say they wanted to first test the atomic bomb. The atomic bomb was dropped on Hiroshima, Japan, August 6, 1945.

284. General George Patton planned to resign and speak out about what was going on behind the scenes of the war. Before he was able to speak to the American people about whatever was on his mind, he was killed in an automobile accident.

285. Germany attacked Poland, which is historically said to be the beginning of World War II on September 1, 1939.

286. September 16, 1939, Russia entered Poland and murdered 10,000 officers of the Polish army.

287. President Roosevelt promised to not involve the American people in World War II if he was elected. But once elected, he formulated a plan to make Japan attack first so he could enter the war without it seeming as if he went back on his word.

288. It was said by some historians that President Roosevelt knew about the war 21 hours prior to Japan bombing Pearl Harbor and that he provoked Japan to war by holding the Pacific fleet in Hawaiian waters as an invitation to that attack.

289. Adolph Hitler was a member of the secret society called the Thule Society (1919).

290. Dietrich Eckart was not only a member of the Thule Society but a high adept, who played a huge part in starting the Nazi Party. He also claimed that he introduced Hitler into the folds of the secret society as well.

291. Some historians say that Hitler was a Jew because his grandmother, Maria Anna Schicklgruber, bore a child from a Rothchild in Vienna, Austria, which was the result of Adolph Hitler's father, Alois Hitler.

292. It was theorized that upon finding out that his lineage may have been of Jewish stock, Hitler went into Austria where he could destroy any evidence of his proposed lineage from Austria's ledgers.

293. The Pima Indians of the Southwestern United States perform a chant in their rituals using Arabic words.

294. The Onandaga Indians of the Iroquois use the honorable title of Eel, which is similar to the title of El commonly used by Moors.

295. Gomara, an explorer, said that an African presence was already in America when the Portuguese arrived.

296. The Navajo, the largest of the North American tribes, possess a symbol called the Naja, which is a crescent moon.

297. The independent state of Morocco was formed in 740 A.D.

298. John D. Rockefeller (1879) was the proud controller of 95% of American oil.

299. John D. Rockefeller was the founder of the General Education Board. It was established in order to give the wealthy of the world real education as opposed to what the masses get.

300. Karl Marx's communist philosophy was free education for all. Some historians say that the education was to be controlled to give the type of information that they felt would best make individuals subservient to the government, thus enabling ones to be a free thinker.

301. One of the objectives of Masonry is to assist man in his growth to inevitably become one with the Omniscient.

302. It is said that the Russians faked the walk in space. They didn't have the technology at the time to accomplish the great feat.

303. The Russian leader Czar Nicholas II oppressed the workers of Russia and that is how some say the Russian Revolution started in 1917. Some say that its cause can be attributed to a competition over oil.

304. The United States assisted Fidel Castro in his career as well as his communist style government.

305. Nikita Khrushcheu, a Russian Communist, said that sooner or later capitalism would give way to socialism (November 16, 1956).

306. Michelangelo was a 15th century Italian architect, sculptor and painter.

307. Some economists promote the propaganda that the world is overpopulated, which absolutely is erroneous. Take the state of Oregon for example, which is 95,607 square miles. The earth's inhabitants (4 billion in 1994) if moved into the state of Oregon, each family of four could fit in a space of approximately 50' by 53'.

308. A woman named Julia Brown spoke out about Dr. Martin Luther King and how he was financed by the communist party and he himself took instructions from them.

309. Leonardo DaVinci was a 15/16th century Italian artist, inventor and scientist.

310. According to the dictionary, *Cultural Literacy 2nd Edition*, revised and updated by E.D. Hirsch, Jr., Joseph F. Kett, James Trefil, Page (131), in reference to Othello, called him a Moor or dark-skinned Moslem.

311. One of the tactics to achieve a new world order that Dr. Brock Chisolm, director of the World Health Organization, explicated that one has to eradicate individualism, loyalty to family tradition, national patriotism and religious dogmas.

312. Niccolo Machiavelli, a prince, promoted the ideology that a prince must use cunning and ruthless methods in order to stay in power.

313. The Bilderbergers are a group of very wealthy and influential men in politics as well as prominent positions in big corporations.

314. Edgar Bronfman, Sr., president of the World Jewish Congress, is a member of the Council on Foreign Relations. At one time, he had 164,000 shares of the Du-Pont common stock.

315. Sir Winston Churchill was the Prime Minister for the English during World War II. Churchill himself has said that there was definitely a world conspiracy at work.

316. Jimmy Carter, who took office as President of the United States in 1936, was a member of the Trilateral Commission.

317. The Rockefeller's dynasty includes many banks, utilities, insurance companies and major industrial corporations.

318. It was once said by a scientist that television was used to control and program the masses. The programming was to suppress the masses ability to think by encouraging their emotions to rule over them.

319. Psychopolitics is the art and science of brainwashing the masses, individuals or bureaucracies.

320. Helena Blavatsky wrote a book, *The Secret Doctrine*, in which she said that the name of the hidden master is "Reason."

321. Meyer Rothchild is the founder of the Rothchild's dynasty. He once said, "Give me the right to issue a nation's money and then I do not care who makes its laws."

322. The real nations of the world are the corporations. Corporations such as AT&T, I.T.T., IBM, DuPONT, DOW, EXXON, TEXACO, GENERAL ELECTRIC, XEROX, ALLIED CHEMICAL, NBC, ABC,CBS, QUAKER OATS, NATIONS BANK, FIAT NYNEX CORP., TIME WARNER, MELLOW BANK, CHRYSLER MOTORS, SEAGRAMS DISTILLING, BOEING AIRCRAFT, PRUDENTIAL INSURANCE, GENERAL MOTORS, LEVI STRAUSS, PEPSICO, GOLDMAN SCHS&CO., and AMERICAN EXPRESS just to name a few.

323. Nelson Rockefeller, on July 26, 1968, said that he would work toward international creation of a new world order based on East-West cooperation instead of conflict. (*The Review of the News;* March 6, 1974)

324. In the city of Philadelphia, 1975, an estimated 60% of black women were using birth control methods in an attempt to prevent conception.

325. A study was done to determine if the health care profession was racially biased toward black women whom used drugs while pregnant as opposed to white women. The study found 15.4% of white women used drugs while pregnant and black women 14.1%. Yet black women were often reported more regularly than white women despite their rate of substance abuse. (*New England Journal of Medicine*)

326. The word "slave" derives from "Slavs," a people subject to the Franks and Jews between 786 and 1009 C.E.

327. The Kaiapo peoples of the Brazilian jungles were the most feared warriors of central Brazil. They are now defending their land from another great conquering warrior – corporations.

328. *The Boston Globe* (April 1972) mentioned a small group of medical students whom performed unnecessary hysterectomies on black patients.

329. In 1855 within the region of Kansa it was a law that punished all black men convicted of rape, attempted rape or kidnapping by castration.

330. European women were a commodity amongst most Moors, Christians and Jewish slavers. They were used as concubines and often placed in Moorish bath houses in North Africa, where they were bought and sold in the marketplace.

331. The war of 1812, started by England against the United States, was for a needed establishment of a central bank in United States from the international bankers.

332. Captain Morgan put out a book exposing the personal insignia of his Free Masonic Order and was later found dead.

333. *Newsweek* once ran an article claiming that black women's drug addiction while pregnant was the cause for the increase in the U.S. infant mortality rate. The charge or claim was completely erroneous due to the fact that the percentage of drug use in white women while pregnant was much higher; yet black women were made the scapegoat for the dilemma.

334. The banking system can create money and credit which gives them power over governments who make policy.

335. Haile Selassie I (born Ras Tafari Makonnen) was overthrown by the Military Junta but the Junta was overthrown later by famine.

336. The airplane was only eleven years old when World War I began. At the end of the war, 177,000 airplanes were used and about 50,000 pilots' lives were sacrificed.

337. The war between China and Japan began in 1937 and ended in 1938. Japan initiated the attack on China, which led to a defeat when Japan captured China's capital.

338. Europeans chose to call themselves white because it was a term that indicated divinity or godliness and also secured their social privileges.

339. The Italians defeated the Abyssinians (Ethiopians) in war 1935-1936. One of the advantages that they had was that they used asphyxiating gas on the people even though this gas was banned at the time by the Geneva Convention.

340. Romulus and Remus, twin brothers, founded the Roman Empire. Both brothers were suckled by a she-wolf. Romulus eventually killed his brother and the Empire of Rome was named after him.

341. The Olmec people of ancient America and the Egyptians or Kemetians both referred to themselves as children of the sun.

342. Europeans were first introduced to the medicinal use of tobacco in Spain by the Moors.

343. Kathy Ferguson said that Clinton was extremely promiscuous. Kathy Ferguson was later found dead as a result of a suicide.

344. Ghana's kings were buried in the style of the ancient Egyptians. They were often buried with their personal belongings.

345. In the year of 876 A.D. the Danes or Vik-Kings were Moorish navigators. Europeans called these Moors Magis sometimes because they were so advanced in technology that they thought the Moors performed magic. When the Moorish Danes went to war, they used cannons and firearms. The Europeans at that time thought it to be fire breathing dragons.

346. (1535) The native people of America, Moors, passed down the science of tobacco to the present day Indians whom use it for spiritual and medicinal purposes.

347. Genghis Khan was 13 when he became the head of a small tribe. Eventually he turned his small tribe into an army that in 1211 began their mission in China to conquer the entire continent. They conquered Russia, Korea, Burma, Vietnam, Iraq and Persia. Genghis Khan passed in the year of 1227.

348. Scientists found traces of cocaine in mummies in Egyptian tombs. The cocoa leaf is grown on the islands close to the Americas, proving it is a possibility that the Egyptians may have been doing trade with the inhabitants of America.

349. Syphilis killed an estimated 10 million people in Europe during the Dark Ages.

350. Suleyman I, the Ottoman Turk, was one of the greatest sultans of the Ottoman Empire. He linked three continents, built fortresses, mosques and other spectacular artifacts during his reign.

351. The people commonly known as Native American Indians in North America as well as the Eskimos in Alaska are "Mongols" that came from the east and are not the original inhabitants of America.

352. The great King Askia Muhammad was the ruler of the Songhay Empire (West Africa) for 35 years. He passed on March 2, 1538.

353. In the 1600's, some Europeans landed in New England. When they landed they found themselves face to face with 700 Moorish natives that went to war with the Europeans for four hours.

354. There are drawings found on clay tablets of men drinking beer through straws as late as 2500 B.C. (Mesopotamia Civilization)

355. (1990) The United States government started the Human Genome Project, a 15-year endeavor to decipher the chemical letters that make up or construct the human DNA alphabet.

356. Jon Parnel Walker, senior investigator for Resolution Trust Corp., was investigating Bill Clinton because of accusations that he was sex crazed. Later he mysteriously fell from a balcony. The verdict was suicide.

357. The illustrious King Juba II of Morocco (25 B.C. – 24 A.D.) married the daughter of Cleopatra, Queen of Egypt. King Juba and the daughter of Cleopatra eventually fled to Ghana because of the Roman overlords' conquest into Morocco. Once they reached Morocco, they began building ships from which they sailed to a continent that is presently called America.

358. In the year 1607, Captain John Smith from England established the first colony in Virginia, America. At the time masonry flourished in England and many men were initiated into the fraternity. One was King James I.

359. Leon 4X Ameer, a close friend of Malcolm X, went to the FBI to file a complaint, with the intent of telling them that the Nation of Islam and the Government had a part in the assassination of Malcolm X. He was killed a couple days later.

360. Katherine Graham, a member of the C.F.R., Bilderbergers, and Trilateral Commission, owns *The Washington Post* newspaper.

361. The Sufi Muslims of Yemen (1450) were some of the first to begin brewing coffee because of its stimulating effects to keep one alert while indulged in nighttime, traditional prayer and meditation.

362. The Columbia Presbyterian Hospital across the street from where Malcolm X was assassinated did not respond to the assassination, so Malcolm X's people had to get the stretcher themselves and help Malcolm.

363. On the *Phil Donahue Show* Jesse Jackson admitted that 20 years ago he had lied about holding Martin Luther King in his arms at his assassination.

364. Julius Cesar of Rome destroyed the Druid altars and the Celtic monuments. He is responsible for building the temples to Apollo, Mars and Venus.

365. Timbuctoo was once known for its lavish and extravagant court, exotic markets, brilliant scholars and civilized citizens. Now, this once great city is in the center of one of the poorest countries in the world.

366. 536 B.C. was the year that the Jews were finally free from subjugation to the Babylonian Empire; Cyrus was the king of Persia.

367. In the year 1312, a group of members from the Knights Templar were under heavy scrutiny by the Pope Clement V. This group of Templars took refuge

because the Pope wanted to persecute them. The Grand Master of the Templars, Jacques De Molay, was later put to death on a cross by the Pope (1314).

368. The Rosetta Stone was found by Napoleon's soldiers as they went into the land of Egypt in 1799. This stone consists of three languages - Egyptian hieroglyphs, Greek and Demotic.

369. The Ottoman Turk, (Mehmed II) Khan Gazi, captured Constantinople in 1453. That was the end of the Byzantine Empire. Authentic documents state that an Amazon Queen from California (America) and her women warriors assisted the Turks in this year as well.

370. William McKinley, Franklin Roosevelt, James Garfield, James Polk, Gerald Ford, Andrew Johnson, Andrew Jackson, Harry Truman, James Buchanan and Warren Harding were presidents of the United States. They were also Masons.

371. The Maasai Tribe has inhabited the Kenya-Tanzania border since the 15th century. The Maasai are known to have been brilliant, fearless, athletic, arrogant, great lovers and wise. They were the most feared warriors in the land at one time.

372. The Toraja people migrated to the island of Sulawesi, Indonesia from Southwest Asia.

373. In the year 1803, a U.S.S. mistakenly went in the direction of Tripoli's harbor. The Barbary pirates of Tripoli held 300 U.S. soldiers captive, making them slaves. Thomas Jefferson sent William Eaton on a mission to wage war on Tripoli but Eaton had to go through many tribulations before he finally gained the assistance of European mercenaries and Bedoin men to defeat the pirates on the shores of Tripoli.

374. Captain Richard Drake, a slave smuggler in the 1830's, said that he made $100,040 selling 250 adults and 100 boys and girls on the Cuban market.

375. The following work is out of Proverbs 22/23 and the teachings of AMEN-EM-OPE, (Pharaoh of Egypt). These two works ironically resemble each other?

Proverbs 22:17-23:14 King Solomon.	Lessons of AMEN-EM-OPE Egyptian Pharaoh.
1. Incline thine ear, and hear my words, and apply thine heart to apprehend; For it is pleasant if thou keep them in thy belly, That they may be fixed like a peg upon they lips.	1. Give thine ear, and hear what I say, and apply thine heart to apprehend; It is good for thee to place them in thine heart, Let them rest in the casket of thy belly. That they may act as a peg upon thy tongue.
2. Have I not written for thee sayings of counsels and knowledge! That thou mayest make known truth to him that speaketh.	2. Consider these thirty chapters; They delight, they instruct. Knowledge how to answer him that speaketh, And how to carry back a report to one that sent him.
3. Rob not the poor for he is a poor, neither oppress the lowly in the gate.	3. Beware of robbing the poor, And of oppressing the afflicted.
4. Associate not with a passionate man, nor go with a wrathful man, lest thou learn his ways and get a snare to thy soul.	4. Associate not with a passionate man, Nor approach him for conversations: Leap not to cleave to such a one, That the terror carry thee not away.
5. A man who is skillful in his business shall stand before kings.	5. A scribe who is skillful in his business, Findeth himself worthy to be a courtier.

"A WISE MAN ONCE SAID THAT TRUTH IS OFTEN STRANGER THAN FICTION"

376. It was once against the law to refuse to grow “hemp” in colonial Virginia (1763 - 1769).

377. The magic mushroom is a plant that Shamans used to alter their state of consciousness. Psilocybin, a substance found in the mushroom, alters the Shamans’ minds to the point where they say that they are able to travel into the infinite realms of the spirit world. Shamans are individuals who possess miraculous superhuman abilities. Shamans are adept in medicine, prognosis of events to come, magical feats and ceremonies. The most popular Shamans are known in Siberia, the Amazon of South American and the Arctic.

378. Statistics show that hallucinogens are abused more by Europeans (whites) than with blacks. Statistics also show that 60% of drug arrests consist of Europeans (whites), yet blacks make up the majority of offenders in prison convicted of drug related offences.

379. George Washington was one of the only presidents to free his slaves. In his will it was stipulated to liberate his slaves upon the death of Martha, his wife.

380. George Lemaitre (1894 - 1966), an astrophysicist, came up with a theory that the stars were originally closer to earth. This was how the big bang theory was brought back to light and is accepted by numerous people today.

381. A near death experience (NDE) is when a person is clinically dead yet has complete awareness of their surroundings as if they were still alive. NDEs have been a controversial subject for over 20 years. In a NDE case, the subject, who

has been diagnosed as deceased, is able to recollect and describe vividly what happened when they were dead upon their recovery.

382. According to ancient Egyptian (kemetic) hieroglyphics, Osiris was conceived by the gods Geb and Nut. Isis, the sister and wife of Osiris, gave birth to their son Horus.

383. November 27, 1830, was the date on which Catherine Laboure said that the spiritual image of the Madonna appeared to her in Paris.

384. The Knights Templar is a fraternity of men who practice esoteric teachings much like that of freemasonry. The organization was founded in 1119 A.D. by warrior monks who banned together in defense of Muslims that sought occupation of their holy land. At that particular time period in France, the Pope forbad any practices of magic or esoteric teachings, which the Knights Templar had been suspected of indulging in. In 1306, Jacques de Molay, the Grand Master of the Knights Templar, met with Pope Clement to discuss the accusations of the Templars performing forbidden practices. Although the Pope did not believe the accusations aimed at Jacques de Molay and the Templars, King Philip the Fair insisted upon the arrest of all Templars, which took place on October 13, 1307. (The present recognition of Friday the 13th is said to derive from this particular event). The Templars that were caught were burned at the stake and the remaining warrior monks went into exile. A few years had passed when 600 Templars later returned to proclaim their innocence of the accusation imposed upon the order of the Knights Templar.

385. Voodoo, originated in West Africa, is based upon the same universal principles that make up the foundation of every religion - cause and effect.

386. The story of Jesus' crucifixion is questionable, as there were 16 other crucified saviors prior to Jesus' birth with the same story as his:

- Thulis of Egypt 1700 B.C.
- Krishna of India 3100 B.C.
- Crite of Chadea 1200 B.C.
- Atys of Phrygia 1170 B.C.
- Thummuz of Syria 1160 B.C.
- Hesus of the Druids 831 B.C.
- Indra of Thibet 725 B.C.
- Bali of Osrissa 725 B.C.
- Iao of Depaul 725 B.C.
- Sakia of India 600 B.C.
- Alcesto of Euripides 600 B.C.
- Mithra of Persia 600 B.C.
- Quexalcote of Mexico 587 B.C.
- Wittoba of the Telingonese 552 B.C.
- Prometheus of Greece 547 B.C.
- Quirinus of Rome 506 B.C.

387. The moon's magnetic force controls the tides of the ocean and is also said to control or rather have influence toward the water based liquid in the brain, which is attributed to heightened emotional states on full moons.

388. The Sadhu of India are men who have vowed to give up all earthly pleasures in order to attain a blissful state of mind. Sadhus are vegetarians, believe in reincarnation and are known to have the ability to perform great feats. These feats are often witnessed by pedestrians include walking on hot coals and blowing fire from their mouths while hot coal is in their mouths. All of these feats are performed without any sign of injury or pain.

389. Before 1883, there were absolutely known laws (federal) permitting the sale, use, manufacture or possession of drugs.

390. In the year of 1994, a priest named Medjugorje, from Civitavecchia in Europe, claimed that a picture of the Black Madonna began to weep tears of blood. The proclaimed bloody tears were tested and to everyone's surprise, the tears were real human blood.

391. Sigmund Freud, a psychologist, excogitated theories which inevitably became the foundation to psychosomatic medicine.

392. Abraham Lincoln once said that prohibition went beyond the bounds of reason in that it attempted to control a man's appetite by legislation, and made a crime out of things that were not crimes.

393. In 1633, astrologist Galileo was ordered to apologize for his theories on the revolution of the earth around the sun as opposed to it being the center of the universe. Instead of being burnt to death for his theories, which were contrary to

popular belief, the Inquisition put him on home confinement for nine years until his subsequent death of natural causes.

394. The Bicentennial Mall located in Nashville, Tennessee, is an exact replica of a 2nd century Chinese manuscript.

395. The epic of Gilamesh is an ancient text found in Mesopotamia and was written 2000 years before the story of Christ.

396. The huge pyramids of the Mayans still exist today in the jungles of Central America. The Mayan civilization began to flourish with their rich culture as early as 350-600 A.D.

397. Captain James Smith (1607) established the first European colony in what is now known as Virginia. Upon his tedious journey he was met with much opposition by the indigenous Moors and Indians. In one particular encounter, he was captured by the indigenous peoples and almost executed, but fate spared his life as a young girl pleaded to her father on his behalf. This young girl was Pocahontas, daughter of the great Al-Gonquin Sachem. On behalf of Pocahontas her father, spared Captain Smith. Pocahontas was only 12 years of age but expressed her emotional desire to become the wife of Captain Smith by professing her love out loud. Pocahontas saved the life of Captain Smith and married him, which some say was a detrimental decision on her behalf. Captain Smith knew that if he married Pocahontas he would inherit legal right to claim the family's wealth and land. Pocahontas relinquished her nobility to gratify her emotional desire which eventually contributed to the destruction of the indigenous civilization of the Moors and Indians. She eventually moved to England with Captain Smith,

changing her name to Rebecca, disregarding her culture and birthright. Pocahontas, unfortunately, passed away at a young age in Europe and Captain John Smith continued in his mission of colonization.

398. James Warren Jim Jones was the leader and founder of The People's Temple, a cult that held beliefs that the end of the world was close and that they needed to sacrifice everything to relinquish their fears of the inevitable. Interestingly, the group's recruited members were poor African Americans and mentally ill people. Some theorized that the members of the group were only subjects of an experiment funded by certain entities. There were claimed reports of the cult members being sexually abused, beaten to death and that they were never permitted to leave the compound at any time. November 20, 1978, 913 members of the People's Temple drank a fruit juice with cyanide poison under the instructions of Jim Jones which terminated their lives. The members of the cult all willingly committed suicide. It is still a mystery to this day as to why 913 men, women and children would execute themselves upon the request of another.

399. Scientists recognized Pluto in 1930 and later realized the possibility of there a tenth planet in the solar system. The ancient master minds of Mesopotamia called this tenth planet the twelfth planet and knew of its existence thousands of years prior to the discovery in 1930.

400. America is one of the most prosperous nations in the world, yet 1.8 million African American youth have no health insurance. Statistically speaking, it is well noted that college graduation is 40% among blacks as opposed to 61% of European (white) students.

401. The Aurora is an aircraft that supposedly can perform amazing feats that would make the average airplane look primitive. Rumors of this craft began to spread around the mid 1980's but the U.S. Department Defense has not made any comments concerning its existence except that its projected creation is expensive to undertake. The SR-71 Blackbird is a spy plane that flew in 1990 and could reach speeds of Mach 3. The Aurora is a craft that is said to do much more than its predecessor.

402. In between the years of 1995 and 2000 there were approximately 10,000 known cases of brutal force on behalf of police officers. Of that, 47.5% are African Americans.

403. There are electronic fish that scientists built to propel through the water at speeds of 50Km/hour.

404. The science of acupuncture was perfected and widely used in the Chinese culture. 400 B.C. is recorded as being the oldest recognized date of acupuncture in the Chinese culture. Part of the basis of acupuncture deals with the Yin and the Yang, which is viewed as two opposing but complementary forces within the body. The Yin represents the feminine force within the body and the Yang is masculine. When these two forces cease to compliment, it causes disturbances and ailments in the body. The practitioner in the science of acupuncture treats the patient by injecting tiny needles in certain points where energy flows. This is done to bring about the unification of those two forces to negate said illness. Europe accepted this science late in the 16th century because of its astronomical results.

405. Amy Robsart was a young lady married to Robert Dudley when Queen Elizabeth rose to the throne and ruled England in 1558. Although Amy Robsart was a faithful wife to her husband, his interest included other ambitions that kept him away from Amy ever so often. Some speculate that he was planning to divorce his wife to gratify the insatiable lust that Queen Elizabeth had for him. Rumors of Queen Elizabeth's attraction to the handsome Robert Dudley were spilling prevalently from the lips of the citizens of London. In the mist of all the gossip, Amy Robsart mysteriously fell from the steps in her home and broke her neck on September 8, 1560. Allegations immediately spread that there was foul play involved. As the years went by Queen Elizabeth and Robert Dudley maintained their innocence. Although it was well recognized that the Queen was indubitably attracted to Dudley, they never married after Amy's death. The Queen eventually dismissed Dudley from her court and reigned as Queen for almost a half a century. The mystery surrounding Amy's death still perplexes the minds of most historians.

ROMAN EMPIRE

406. The Roman Empire reigned from 753 B.C. to 476 A.D. and is often held as one of the most historically accomplished civilizations in its time. Although it can be concluded that this may be a matter of opinion, the fact still remains that the Roman Empire's architectural and governmental structure has influenced modern civilizations of today. In Washington D.C., the Jefferson Memorial splendidly reflects the Pantheon that stood in the Roman Republic 1700 years ago. Ancient

Rome was strongly influenced by the Greek civilization, whom was influenced by the Egyptian (Kemet) culture.

POPULAR ROMAN GENERALS

Publius Cornelius Scipio Africanus (235 - 183 B.C.)

Galus Marius (158 - 87 B.C.)

Lucius Cornelius Sulla (138 - 79 B.C.)

Pompey (106 - 48 B.C.)

Julius Caesar (101 - 44 B.C.)

Mark Antony (83 - 30 B.C.)

Marcus Agrippa (63 - 12 B.C.)

Nero Drusus (40 - 9 B.C.)

Galus Julius Agricola (40 - 93 A.D.)

Germanicus (15 B.C. – 19 A.D.)

407. Rome was named after Romulus, founder of the Roman Empire. Romulus was said to have been given a divine sign previous to establishing his empire which entailed of twelve eagles that came down from heaven. Some scholars have interpreted this divine sign as an allegorical astrological meaning that his empire would reign for 1200 years. It is not strange that Romulus' empire stood strong for 1229 years.

ROMAN EMPERORS

Romulus 753 B.C.

Numa Pompilius 716 B.C.

Tullus Hostilius 673 B.C.

Ancus Marcius 640 B.C.

L. Tarquinius Priscus 616 B.C.

Servius Tullius 578 B.C.

Fabius Maximus 217 B.C.

Tiberius Gracchus 133 B.C.

Gaius Gracchus 123 B.C.

Sulla 82 B.C.

Caesar 46 B.C.

Augustus 27 B.C.

Tiberius I 14 C.E.

Caligula 37 C.E.

Nero 54 C.E.

Galba 68 C.E.

Galba; Otha, Vitellius 69 C.E.

Vespasianus 69 C.E.

Titus 79 C.E.

Domitianus 81 C.E.

Nerva 98 C.E.

Trajanus 93 C.E.

Hadrianus 117 C.E.

Antonius Pius 138 C.E.

Marcus Aurelius and Lucius Verus 161 C.E.

Marcus Aurelius 169 C.E.

Commodus 180 C.E.

Pertinax; Julianus I 193 C.E.

Septimius Severus 193 C.E.

Caracalla and Geta 211 C.E.

Caracalla 212 C.E.

Macrinus 217 C.E.

Elagaballus 218 C.E.

Alexander Severus 222 C.E.

Maximus I 235 C.E.

Gordianus I and Gordianus II, Pupienus and Balbinus 235 C.E.

Gordianus III 235 C.E.

Philippus 244 C.E.

Decius 249 C.E.

Gallus and Volusianus 251 C.E.

Aemilianus 253 C.E.

Valerianus and Gallienus 253 C.E.

Gallienus 258 C.E.

Claudius Gothicus 268 C.E.

Quintillus 270 C.E.

Aurelianus 270 C.E.

Tacitus 275 C.E.

Florianus 276 C.E.

Probus 276 C.E.

Carus 282 C.E.

Carinus and Numerianus 283 C.E.

Diocletianus and Maximianus 286 C.E.

Galerius and Constantius I 305 C.E.

Galerius, Maximinus II, Severus I 306 C.E.

Galerius, Maximinus II, Constantinus I, Licinius, Maxentius 307 C.E.

Maximinus II, Constantinus I, Licinius, Maxentius 311 C.E.

Maximinus II, Constantinus I, Licinius 314 C.E.

Constantinus I and Licinius 314 C.E.

Constantinus I (The Great) 324 C.E.

Constantinus II, Constans I, Constantinus II 337 C.E.

Constantinus II and Constans I 340 C.E.

Constantinus II 350 C.E.

Julianus II 361 C.E.

Jovianus 363 C.E.

ROME (East)

Valentinianus I 364 C.E.

Valentinianus I and Gratianus 367 C.E.

Gratianus and Valentinianus II 374 C.E.

Gratianus and Valentinianus II 378 C.E.

Valentinianus II 383 C.E.

Theodosius I 394 C.E.

Honorius 395 C.E.

Honorius 408 C.E.

Valentinianus III 423 C.E.

Valentinianus III 450 C.E.

Maximus and Avitus 455 C.E.

Avitus 456 C.E.

Majorianus 457 C.E.

Severus II 461 C.E.

Anthemius 467 C.E.

Olybrius 472 C.E.

Glycerius 473 C.E.

Julius Nepos 474 C.E.

Romulus Augustulus 475 C.E.

476 C.E. (End of Empire)

CONSTANTINOPLE (WEST)

Valens 363 C.E.

Valens 367 C.E.

Valens 375 C.E.

Theodosius 378 C.E.

Theodosius 383 C.E.

Theodosius I 394 C.E.

Arcadius 395 C.E.

Theodosius II 408 C.E.

Theodosius II 423 C.E.

Marcianus 450 C.E.

Marcianus 455 C.E.

Marcianus 456 C.E.

Leo I 457 C.E.

Leo I 461 C.E.

Leo I 467 C.E.

Leo I 472 C.E.

Leo I 473 C.E.

Leo I 474 C.E.

Zeno 475 C.E.

476 C.E. (End of Empire)

EGYPTIAN DYNASTIC PHAROAHS AND QUEENS

1st Dynasty
Narmer 3200-2980 B.C.

II Dynasty
Neter-baiu 2980 2900 B.C.

III Dynasty
Djoser, Humi 2720-2700 B.C.

IV Dynasty
Sneferu, Khufu
Khafra, Men-kau-Ra 2680-2565 B.C.

V Dynasty
Nefer-f-Ra, Tet-kau-Ra, 2565-2420 B.C.
Unas

VI Dynasty
Teta, Usr-ka-Ra,
Pepi I, Mernere 2420-2270 B.C.

VII, VIII, IX & X Dynasty
Nefer-ka, Ab, Nefer-ka-Ra
Nefer-ka-ari-Ra 2270-2100 B.C.

XI Dynasty
Antef II 2150-2090 B.C.
Antef III 2090-2085 B.C.
Mentuhotep I 2085-2065 B.C.
Mentuhotep II 2065-2060 B.C.
Mentuhotep III 2060-2015 B.C.
Mentuhotep IV 2015-2005 B.C.
Mentuhotep V 2005-2000 B.C.

XII Dynasty
Amenehat I 2000-1979 B.C.
Senwosret I 1970-1936 B.C.
Amenohat II 1938-1904 B.C.
Senworset II 1906-1888 B.C.
Senworset III 1888-1850 B.C.
Amenohat III 1850-1800 B.C.
Amenohat IV 1800-1972 B.C.

XIII Dynasty

Xu-taiu-Ra,
Semen-ka-Ra
Sebek-hetep I,
Xa-hetep-Ra
Xerp-uah-xa-Ra 1785- ? B.C.

<u>XIV Dynasty</u>
Ner-nefer-Ra
Te-xeru-Ra 1675 - ? B.C.

<u>XV Dynasty</u>
As-peh-Set,
Apepa 1675-1600 B.C.

<u>XVI Dynasty</u>
As-ab-taiu-Ra Ra 1600-1600 B.C.

<u>XVII Dynasty</u>
Seqenen-Ra, Kamose 1600-1580 B.C.

<u>XVIII Dynasty</u>
Ahmose I 1580-1558 B.C.
Amenhotep I 1557-1530 B.C.
Thutomose I 1530-1515 B.C.
Hatshepsut "The Great Queen" 1515-1484 B.C.
Thutmose III 1504-1450 B.C.
Amenhotep II 1450-1415 B.C.
Thutmose IV 1415-1405 B.C.
Amenhotep III and Queen Tiyi 1405-1370 B.C.
Amenhotep IV and Queen Nefer-ti-ti 1370-1352 B.C.
Tut-ankh-Amen ? -1352 B.C.

<u>XIX Dynasty</u>
Harembeb 1340-1320 B.C.
Rameses I 1320-1318 B.C.
Seti I 1318-1298 B.C.
Ramese II 1298-1232 B.C.

<u>XX Dynasty</u>
Merneptah 1232-1224 B.C.
Setinekht 1200-1198 B.C.
Ramese III 1198-1168 B.C.

<u>XXI Dynasty</u>
Ra-neter-xeper 1085-950 B.C.

XXII Dynasty
Sheshonq 950-920 B.C.
Osorkon I 925-893 B.C.
Takhlet I 893-870 B.C.
Osorkon II 870-847 B.C.
Takhlet II 847-823 B.C.
Sheshonq II 823-772 B.C.

XXIII Dynasty
Se-her-ab-Ra,
Ra-setep-Amen 772-718 B.C.

XXIV Dynasty
Kashta, Piankhi 718-718 B.C.

XXV Dynasty
Piankhi 718-716 B.C.
Shabakha 716-701 B.C.
Shabatakha 701-690 B.C.
Taharkha 690-664 B.C.
Tanutemun 664-653 B.C.

XXVI Dynasty
Psenthek I 663-609 B.C.
Necho 609-594 B.C.
Psemthek II 594-588 B.C.
Apries 588-568 B.C.
Amasis 568-527 B.C.

XXVII Dynasty
Cambyses, Darius 527-404 B.C.

XXVIII Dynasty
Semen-en-Ptah-mentu-setep 409-399 B.C.

XXIX Dynasty
Ba-en-Ra-neteru-meri 399-378 B.C.

XXX Dynasty
Necatanebos I 378-360 B.C.
Nectanebos II 360-341 B.C.

XXXI Dynasty
????????? 341-332 B.C.

XXXII Dynasty

Alexander II 332-323 B.C.
(The Great)

<u>XXXIII Dynasty</u>
Soter I (Ptolemy I) 323-283 B.C.
Ptolemy II-XIII 283-244 B.C.
Cleopatra VIII (The Queen) 244-30 B.C.

<u>XXXIV Dynasty</u>
Suten net Au,
Caesar Augustus, Tiberias etc. 30-324 B.C.

Egypt is a Greek word which is a distorted name of the pyramid civilization existing in the northeastern sector of Africa originally called KMT or Kamit. Kamit means the," land of the Blacks". The dynastic period of Kamit as proposed by modern scholars is sadi to have began between 4,000/3,000 B.C. However, The archeological evidence found throughout ancient and modern Kamit places this high cultured civilizations history beyond the dynastic period intertwining with the culture of Atlantis which was a civilization existing between what is now known the Atlantic Ocean around 39,000BC. Manetho300B.C., a Kamitic high priest spoke of the existence of Atlantis as well as the Greek philosopher plato, who received his education from kamit(Egypt). The ancient kamitic people, along with their relatives from Atlantis felt that man or woman had two aspects that composed themselves. The consciousness, which is responsible for willed behavior and the unconsciousness(subcounscious/spirit) which is associated with involuntary actions such as the workings of internal organs within the human body. In kamitic mystic spiritual pratctices, it is the duty of every human being to unifythe two aspects of themselves, to become one with the divine spirit, their divine nature. In doing so one becomes a living replica of god, enabling them to use their natural but dormant faculties which include telepathy, claircoyance, levitation, telekenisis, astral projection and E.S.P. to fulfill their lifes purpose. Refer to Andrew Collins, Beneath the Pyramids, Cgristopher Dunn/ Lost Technologies of ancient Egypt and Edward Malkowski/ Ancient Egypt 39,000B.C.

THE CIVIL WAR

It is theorized that European bankers were the initial agitators behind the Civil War. They wanted to establish a national bank in America but they knew that the American people would protest so they decided to begin plotting on how they could start a war with the United States and another country. This would put both countries in a position where they would have to borrow money to finance the war effort on their behalf, which would leave them subject as debtors to pay back what they borrowed and then the international bankers could implement their plot to create a national bank in the United States. The European bankers decided to split the Union by creating dissension between the North and South. They came up with an issue of slavery and established an organization in the South called the Knights of the Golden Circle that would be able to promote this ideal. The southern states would then separate themselves from the Union and form the Confederation of States, which would be all sovereign states. April 12, 1861, the Civil War began in South Carolina at Fort Sumter. Abraham Lincoln, at the time, realized that the war wasn't really about slavery but an attempt to split up the Union. He realized that there was a power greater than the southern states behind the whole thing and knew that England as well as France were siding with the southern states.

Abraham Lincoln was still reluctant to borrow money from the bankers so he created the "green back," which was money that was debt free and backed by nothing. The European bankers were furious with Lincoln's efforts at issuing out green backs because it was destroying the bankers' initial plot to create a national bank and loan the government money. The Europeans from England and France closed in on Lincoln by deploying troops into Canada from England and the French troops whom were on the outskirts of Mexico. Lincoln's whole objective was simply to save the Union and he said out of his own mouth, "If I could save the Union without freeing any slaves, I would do it." The Congress eventually passed the National Banking Act, February 25,

1863. Now there was going to be a federally charted bank that loaned the government U.S. notes that were backed by debt. With England and France supporting the South it added a heap of pressure on the North. So Lincoln found an ally that had a powerful navy and was feared by both England and France and that was Russia. Lincoln passed the Emancipation Proclamation only to impress the Russians because they themselves had recently just freed the serfs and Lincoln thought that this would prompt the Russians to subside with the United States and send their naval force to the assistance of the North. Thus, the Russians came to the aid of the North and the slaves in the United States were physically freed from bondage. Lincoln's fear was not that England, France and the southern states were insistent upon going to war, but Lincoln feared that the demise of the country would diminish at the hands of an internal threat far greater.

Lincoln also often had visions of his own assassination that eventually came to a reality on April 14, 1865. His assassin was a man named John Wilkes Booth. The North eventually won the war and the South was allowed to become part of the Union under certain stipulations, which included that they pay back the debt for the war on both sides. Lincoln's plan had worked because in the end the European bankers still couldn't establish the central bank in the United States, yet.

"THE MONEY POWERS PREY UPON THE NATION IN TIMES OF PEACE AND CONSPIRES AGAINST IT IN TIMES OF ADVERSITY."

Abraham Lincoln

WORLD WAR I

It is commonly suggested amongst some historians that the real reason behind World War I was to establish a world government which was to be a conglomerate of nations that would unite in order to prevent the outbreak of future wars. This collaboration of nations was to be called the League of Nations. It seems evident that

World War I was preplanned for the purpose of bringing about this agenda five years prior to the assassination of Archduke Francis Ferdinand on June 28, 1914. In 1909 there was a proposed meeting amongst the Committee to Investigate Tax Exempt Foundations, which was a part of the United States House of Representatives. Norman Dodd, the director, exclaimed that the topic was how the American people's lives could be altered, and the reply was through war. It was in their interest now to create a method from which the United States could become involved in the war between Germany and England/France. One of the strangest paradoxes in this whole war is how 121 American people were killed when the Lusitania ship was bombed in the English Channel. This ship was sent to New York and then stocked with millions of rounds of ammunition in order to assist England/France in their war endeavors toward Germany. The ocean liner was set to sail with the ammunition and American passengers who were designated to England.

It is well noted historically that the government of Germany warned America by placing an advertisement in the newspapers not to board the ship because it was going to sail through a war zone. President Woodrow Wilson was also warned but did nothing to alert the American people. This was said to be the method in which they were constructing to enter the United States into the war. The conspires theorized that when the Lusitania sailed into the war zone it would be destroyed along with the American people, which would then give the United States probable cause to enter the war. May 7, 1915, the Lusitania was sunk by a German boat. After the war ended November 11, 1918, there was created a treaty by the conquering nations in order to prevent any future war. But this treaty was not perpetual and was only a 20-year truce. The League of

Nations Charter was also signed by Woodrow Wilson, but like the treaty, it was not ratified when presented by Woodrow Wilson because of the American people's dissatisfaction in having long-term relations with foreign nations. The plot to establish a world government was thus unsuccessful. Warren G. Harding was elected president after Woodrow Wilson. President Harding later died due to health complications but many believe that he was eliminated because he opposed the plan to establish a world government by the conspiratorial powers.

WORLD WAR II

It was theorized that World War II was agitated due to the fact that World War I was unsuccessful in establishing a world government. World War II gave birth to the United Nations, which like the League of Nations, was established to prevent future war and bring about a new world order of peace amongst the nation. September 1, 1939, Germany attacked Poland, which was the beginning of World War II. Prior to

Germany's attack, Adolf Hitler, Germany's Nazi dictator, invaded Austria, which was said to be what initially started World War II. Historians have said that Hitler wanted to invade Austria to destroy records that would show evidence of his Jewish ancestry or lineage. This theory was taken into consideration due to the allegations that Adolf Hitler's father, Alois Hitler, was the son of Baron Rothchild whom fecundated Maria Anna Schicklgruber. Maria was a housekeeper in the house of Baron Rothchild and when she was found to be pregnant she was relieved of her duties and sent to Spitol where she gave birth to Alois Hitler. Adolf Hitler was not at all happy about his supposed lineage of Jewish ancestry because his agenda at the time was to destroy all Jews, Blacks and other ethnic groups, so that he could promote his white supremacy Nazi party ideology. Hitler was in the business of creating a new race that would be a blond hair blue eye race which would rule the earth. Adolf Hitler was very successful at exterminating the lives of many.

One weapon that he used to carry out his mission of death was a lethal gas called Zyklon B. A company named I.G. Farben manufactured this gas and obtained the capital to do so from Wall Street. I.G. Farben controlled the assets of I.G. Farben. The board of directors consisted of a panel of a majority of Americans, one of whom was Charles E. Mitchell, President of Rockefeller's National City Bank of New York. This is not strange at all; in fact, there were American oil companies supplying Germany during the war. President Roosevelt, like Woodrow Wilson, promised the American people that he would not get the American people involved in the war. Behind closed doors, President Roosevelt found a way that he could enter into the war without breaking his promise. Germany's allies were Italy and Japan, which meant that if Roosevelt could find a way to provoke one of Germany's allies to attack first, he could enter into the war out of defense for his country. President Roosevelt made sure that they would give aid to the Dutch and English by oil shipments, which would instigate Japan to attack and give the United States probable cause to enter the war. Japan eventually attacked the American navy at Pearl Harbor. It is theorized that President Roosevelt knew before hand of this surprise attack. One reason that this theory is entertained within the minds of some historians is that a Japanese message was decoded by the American government which basically said that Japan was going to attack the U.S. This telegram was given to President Roosevelt but he did nothing to alert the navy at Pearl Harbor. Roosevelt made sure that the attack would be successful by ordering the aircrafts at Pearl Harbor to face each other so that when the attack was initiated the aircrafts would not be able to retaliate quickly enough. Japan attacked Pearl Harbor December 7, 1941. December 8, 1941, President Roosevelt declared war on Japan. December 11, 1941, Germany declared war on the United States. Fifty nations eventually signed a declaration. "Thus we have the beginning of a new world order."

CONCLUSIONS ON WAR

Every experience in life is suppose to be didactic for the fortification of our mind and character, even if the experience is an extraordinary as the war of Vietnam (1964-1975). Being that I am the son of an 82nd Airborn Ranger whom survived this traumatic war, my observation of its psychological ramifications are first hand. The war itself was not only traumatic but the aftermath that showed its presence upon the soldiers return to

America was even more horrific. In retrospect, I can just imagine how it must have felt for my father upon his return to America, only to find no embrace from the same country he had just fought for. Although the strain of adversity seemed overwhelming at the particular point, it ignited the flame of determination needed to succeed and overcome those same obstacles that opposed his passage. Everyone in life will experience WAR, weather it is physically, mentally and/or both simultaneously; we must realize that the ultimate war is a battle fought within one's own self. The determination to excel to higher heights is guided by the force of one's will and the wise man will use adverse situations as motivational fuel to fortify his will in overcoming his undesired reality. The primary objective of war throughout history has been to conquer or to bring the enemy into subjugation of the WILL, which is very ironic since man has been engaged in a battle similar within his own mind. Man will forever fight in bloody wars until one day he 'awakens' to find that his only enemy is his own great self.

KNOW THY SELF

PEACE

ABOUT THE AUTHOR

Akiba Rakilam-EL has been sedulously engrossed with the retrieving and exposing of publicly hidden facts for well over a decade. His investigative expertise has lead to the mass accumulation of eccentric based information. He currently gives lectures throughout the northeast and southeast regions of the United States.

Points of Reference

All the facts within this book are supported by the following references:

Fact Number(s) - 319, 314, 77, 88, 91, 320

- Akiba Rakilam-EL/Little Book of Essential Knowledge

Fact Number(s) - 345, 47

- Michael A Hoffman/Egypt Before the Pharaohs

Fact Number(s) – 119, 83, 82

- H. St. John Philby/ The Queen of Sheba

Fact Number(s) – 345, 186, 129, 122, 116, 97, 76

- Margaret Shinne/ Ancient African Kingdoms

Fact Number(s) – 135, 101

- Robert Temple/ The Sirius Mystery

Fact Number(s) – 345, 200, 177, 170, 164, 156, 108, 107, 76, 47

- Scott Wayne/ Egypt & the Sudan

Fact Number(s) -135

- Ivan T. Sanderson/ Investigating the Unexplained

Fact Number(s) – 186, 129, 97

- David Hatcher Childress/ Lost Cities & Ancient Mysteries of Africa & Arabia

Fact Number(s) – 374, 206, 202, 124, 80, 75

- James Grey Jackson/ An Account of the Empire of Morocco

Fact Number(s) – 295, 294, 207, 56

- Jack Forbes/ Black Africans and Native Americans
- Wesley Jones/ A Critical Study of the Book of Mormon Sources

Fact Number(s) - 153

- J.A. Rogers/ 100 Amazing Facts About the Negro

Fact Number(s) - 56

- Gomez/ The Journal of Southern History

Fact Number(s) - 153

- Richard B. Moore/ The Name "Negro," It's Origin and Evil Use

Fact Number(s) – 294, 207, 153, 56

- J. Leirch Wright Jr./ Creeks and Seminoels

Fact Number(s) - 153

- J.A. Rogers/ Sex and Race

Fact Number(s) - 153

- J.A. Rogers/ Nature Knows No Color Line

Fact Number(s) – 350, 347, 343, 251, 214, 206, 204, 202, 201, 130, 124, 75

- E.W. Bovill/ The Golden Trade of the Moors
- Carter G. Woodson/ Miseducation of the Negro

Fact Number(s) – 374, 350, 347, 343, 298, 206, 204, 202, 130, 124, 80, 75

- Van Sertima/ Golden Age of the Moors

Fact Number(s) – 212, 109, 11

- Mac Ritchie/ Ancient & Modern Briton Vol II

Fact Number(s) – 298, 297, 295, 294, 227, 72, 37, 26, 10

- Jose V. Pimienta-Bey, Ph. D/ Othello's Children in the New World, Moorish History & Identity in the African American Experience
- Brewton Berry/ Almost White

Fact Number(s) – 366, 85

- Felix Dubois/ Timbuctoo the Mysterious

Fact Number(s) - 367

- Soloman Grayzel/ A History of the Jews
- Clark John Ridpath/ Universal History

Fact Number(s) - 367

- Hiam Elias Lindo/ The History of the Jews of Spain and Portugal

- John P. Burnell/ The Guineas of West Virginia

Fact Number(s) – 366, 85, 21

- Rudolph R. Windsor/ From Babylon Timbuctu

Fact Number(s) - 48

- George Rawlinson/ The History of Herdotus

Fact Number(s) – 407, 365, 341, 256, 227, 226, 211, 112, 111, 106, 84

- Edward Gibson/ The Decline and Fall of the Roman Empire
- John Blessingame/ The Slave Community

Fact Number(s) – 281, 216, 104

- Nahum Slouscher/ Travels in North Africa
- Joseph Deniker/ The Races of Mankind
- Cecil Roth/ A History of the Marranos

Fact Number(s) – 386, 175, 97

- Joseph Williams/ Hebrewism of West Africa
- James Bruce/ Travels to Discover the Source of the Nile

Fact Number(s) - 61

- Horace Leonard Jones/ The Geography of Strabo

Fact Number(s) – 371, 265

- Oscar Jewell Harvey/ A History of Lodge #61, F and A.M.

Fact Number(s) – 371, 333, 265

- W.L. Wilmuhurst/ The Meaning of Masonry

Fact Number(s) - 109

- Samuel Scott/ The History of the Moorish Empire in Europe
- David Brion Davis/ The Fear of Conspiracy
- Gary Allen/ The Rockefeller file
- Robert Goldstone/ The Russian Revolution
- Rene Fulop-Miller/ The Power and Secret of the Jesuits
- Colin Simpson/ The Lusitania
- Guy Richardson/ The Hunt for Czar
- Admiral Robert/ The Final Secret of Pearl Harbor
- Albert Mackey/ An Encyclopedia of Freemasonry
- Treavor Ravenscroft/ The Spear of Destiny
- John Robison/ Proofs of Conspiracy
- Donzella Cross Boyle/ Quest of a Hemisphere
- Nathaniel Weyl/ Red Star over Cuba
- Robert Welch/ The Politician
- Leonid Vladimirov/ The Russian Space Bluff
- Emmanuel Josephson/ The Federal serve Conspiracy and the Rockefellers
- Matthew Hale/ The History of the Common Law of England
- Benjamin Freedman/ Facts are Facts
- John Coleman/ Diplomacy by Deception: An Account of the Treasonous Conduct by the Government of Britain and the United States
- William Cooper/ Behold a Pale Horse
- David H. Lewis/ Days before Tomorrow

- Dess Griffin/ Descent into Slavery
- Baigent, Leigh & Lincoln/ Holy Blood Holy Grail
- E Szekely/ The Essene Gospel of Peace Book one
- Dr. Frank Barr/ Melanin the Organizing Molecule
- Mantak Chia/ Awaken Healing Energy Through the Tao
- David Childress/ The lost Continent of Mu
- Van Sertima/ Blacks In Science
- G. Higgins/ Anacalypsis
- Marcel Griaule/ Conversations with Ogotemmeli
- Ersky Freeman/ 1001 Black Inventions
- Pro. Frederick Soddy/ Wealth, Virual Wealth & debt
- Barbara Villiers/ History of Money Crimes
- Jon Rappoport & David Icke/ Lifting the Veil
- Rudolph Steiner/ Philosophy of Freedom
- Dr. John Coleman/ What You Should Know About the U.S. Constitution
- William Moseley/ Highlights of Templar History
- Manly P. Hall/ The Phoenix
- David Icke/ I am me, I am Free
- Sidney Warburg/ Hitler's Secret Backers
- Nesta H. Webster/ World Revolution: The Plot Against Civilization
- Nesta Webster/ Germany and the Jews
- Gary Allen/ None Dare Call It Conspiracy
- Vera Stanley Alder/ When Humanity Comes of Age

- Gary Allen/ Federal Reserve: The Trillion Dollar Conspiracy
- Vicomte Leon de Poncins/ State Secrets
- Antony Sutton/ America's Secret Establishment: Introduction to the Order of the Skull & Bones

www.ingramcontent.com/pod-product-compliance
Ingram Content Group UK Ltd.
Pitfield, Milton Keynes, MK11 3LW, UK
UKHW041933190726
13854UKWH00004B/1556

9 781257 108015